Middle Schools FOR A Diverse Society

"The book is inspiring and renders an authentic and experienced fresh voice in middle school literature. The sincere honesty and sharing as a White female educator provides a different voice in the contemporary diversity literature that should be included among all scholarly work in multicultural education and middle school learning. Kathleen Chamberlain provides another view in the expanding area of Whiteness studies and multicultural education. This book should be included on the shelves of all educators as a resource that draws upon compassion and provides different perspectives in curriculum theory, critical theory, feminist theory, and constructivism from an autobiographical perspective."

Andrew Jackson, Sr., Academic Advisor
and Instructor of Education, College of Education,
The Pennsylvania State University; President of the Pennsylvania
Chapter and Director of Region Three
of the National Association for Multicultural Education

"Kathleen Chamberlain has written a passionate and informative book that provides the groundwork for looking deeply at preparing middle schools for a diverse society. She argues for school-wide and individual changes in our conceptualization of middle school education, which should begin with dialogues. As conversations surrounding middle school education gain prominence across the nation, this book will serve as a stimulus for all stakeholders."

Ruth McKoy Lowery, University of Florida;
Author of Immigrants in Children's Literature (Lang, 2000)

MIDDLE SCHOOLS

FOR A

DIVERSE SOCIETY

Studies in the
Postmodern Theory of Education

Joe L. Kincheloe and Shirley R. Steinberg
General Editors

Vol. 241

PETER LANG
New York • Washington, D.C./Baltimore • Bern
Frankfurt am Main • Berlin • Brussels • Vienna • Oxford

Kathleen Chamberlain

MIDDLE
SCHOOLS
FOR A
DIVERSE
SOCIETY

PETER LANG
New York • Washington, D.C./Baltimore • Bern
Frankfurt am Main • Berlin • Brussels • Vienna • Oxford

Library of Congress Cataloging-in-Publication Data

Chamberlain, Kathleen.
Middle schools for a diverse society / Kathleen Chamberlain.
p. cm. — (Counterpoints; v. 241)
Includes bibliographical references and index.
1. Multicultural education—United States. 2. Middle school
education—United States. I. Title. II. Counterpoints
(New York, N.Y.); v. 241.
LC1099.3.C46   372.24'2—dc21   2002156040
ISBN 0-8204-6370-1
ISSN 1058-1634

Bibliographic information published by **Die Deutsche Bibliothek**.
Die Deutsche Bibliothek lists this publication in the "Deutsche
Nationalbibliografie"; detailed bibliographic data is available
on the Internet at http://dnb.ddb.de/.

Cover design by Sophie Boorsch Appel

The paper in this book meets the guidelines for permanence and durability
of the Committee on Production Guidelines for Book Longevity
of the Council of Library Resources.

© 2003 Peter Lang Publishing, Inc., New York
275 Seventh Avenue, 28th Floor, New York, NY 10001
www.peterlangusa.com

Printed in the United States of America

For Macy Rebekah

May she learn in a world of peace and understanding

TABLE OF CONTENTS

Acknowledgments ix
Introduction.. 1

1   Understandings... 5
2   Developmental Responsiveness...21
3   Identity.. 39
4   Success 55
5   Relationships... 73
6   Community.. 91
7   Dialogues 109
8   Flexibility and Change 127
9   Recommended Reading.. 143

Bibliography... 151
Index 161

ACKNOWLEDGMENTS

I would like to express my gratitude to those who supported me through all my efforts. First, I thank my husband, Bill, who helped me realize my dreams. I cannot forget my sons, Chris and Matthew, who lived through my "mom the student" days and brought me much joy. I also want to thank Rachael Hungerford, my Department Chair, who encouraged me to believe in myself as a writer. Finally, I want to thank Joe Kincheloe and Shirley Steinberg, the series editors, who introduced me to the concepts of critical theory and encouraged me to explore my own assumptions and beliefs.

INTRODUCTION

One may question the rationale for a middle-aged, white, female educator from a rural northeastern community writing a book about diversity. In fact, I questioned myself as I was preparing this work. I did not grow up in a diverse community nor have I had extensive work with other cultures. However, I am an example of the kind of person for whom this book is written. American schools are becoming more diverse, and teachers of young adolescents are dealing with issues related to adolescent development compounded by increased diversity among students. Rural America will not continue to be isolated from diversity issues.

Education is a political issue; standards and tests scores are often in the news. Teachers and students are being tested, and funding is based upon how well students do on standardized tests. The solution for violence and unrest in schools is money for band-aids: metal detectors, police and probation officers in schools, and "just say no" type programs. Missing from the conversations is a discussion of students and the environment in which they interact on a day-to-day basis. Those who attempt to address student issues are chided that their work doesn't have statistically verifiable results. Student interpersonal growth takes time and energy. Sometimes, the results don't appear until years later. I have heard the problems in education being blamed on the *progressive* movement during which teachers supposedly no longer teach and students just learn what they want. Such reformers are sure that if we just get back to basics, the ills of society will be cured. Nothing could be farther from the truth.

Critics of public education have basic assumptions to support their assertion that schools are failing. Schools are not failing. Yes, there are problems; nothing is perfect. Teachers are anxious to do a good job; they may be frustrated and need support. Students are not lazy and unable to learn; kids are actually quite knowledgeable. Student-centered classrooms and high standards can co-exist. I hope to challenge the negative assumptions about life in a middle school and promote a problem-solving attitude.

Information in this book is based upon my thirty-plus years as an educator and my doctoral dissertation, *Student Perceptions of Their Middle School Learning Environment* for which I did extensive research about middle school philosophy, adolescent development, and learning environments. As part of that research, I surveyed middle school students and teachers and conducted student focus groups. That study led me to more in-depth investigations of adolescent issues.

This is a book about growth and change. It is intended to provoke discussion and action. This book contains a mixture of theory and practice. I use examples from my own experience to illustrate issues. Often, when I walk into work, colleagues remark that I always seem to be smiling. I guess I do smile most of the time. I smile because I truly like my work as a teacher. I believe that it is a great responsibility to work with pre-service teachers who will be entering the profession as middle school and high school teachers. As I work with my students, I find that many of them, like me, did not have experiences in diverse communities. They struggle with their assumptions and beliefs about culture as I did.

Readers may connect to the text with examples of their own. I hope they do. Chapter 1 traces the evolution of my personal perspective of middle schools for a diverse society. Within the chapter, I propose challenges for middle level educators and situate these challenges in a theoretical perspective. This chapter "sets the stage" for subsequent chapters and encourages readers to reflect upon their own experiences and assumptions. Chapter 2 reviews developmental theories, learning environment theories, and the philosophy of middle level education as proposed by major theorists and organizations.

In Chapter 3, I propose that a challenge for educators is to provide learning experiences that promote the development of a student's individual identities as a learner; member of the family, school, or community; and as a friend. This chapter will encourage the reader to look at the concept of identity through multiple perspectives.

Chapter 4 includes discussions of the meaning of success and how perceptions of success impact upon classroom practice and student achievement. Another challenge that I propose is the challenge for educators to provide opportunities for students to interact with peers and adults showing care, respect, and trust. Chapter 5 encourages educators to consider aspects of learning environments that support the development of positive relationships.

Chapter 6 challenges readers to consider their ideas about community and democracy. Also addressed is the concept of citizenship and how it is developed in curriculum and school practices. Student participation in decision-making and the roles all take in the community are discussed.

Chapter 7 emphasizes the importance of talking with students in a changing school community. I will distinguish between talking "to" students and talking "with" students. Communication among all stakeholders in the community will be explored.

Chapter 8 proposes that educators who wish to provide schools to meet the needs of young adolescents in a diverse society must look to the future; they must be agents of change. Finally, Chapter 9 includes an annotated bibliography of books that I found helpful in developing my understandings.

As schools move into a new century, unknown challenges will face educators from inside our own country and the world. Through science, options for life choices will expand. Ethics and understanding of others will be even more important. We cannot forget our past and the forces that have molded who and what we are. Nevertheless, we cannot look to the past for all our answers. We must look to today as a portal to the future. Moving ahead will not be easy. We will be faced with tests that no one has predicted and not all current solutions will work. Resilient teachers and students will meet the challenge.

I have been fortunate to have friends who have shared their stories and concerns with me. Through their friendship and honesty, I am a "work in progress." I am an optimist; I know schools will get better. I am a believer in people; I know they are resilient. I am a learner; there is so much more to learn. I am a teacher.

CHAPTER 1

Understandings

Like many teachers, I looked at *Open House Night* at school as a time when I had to make sure every student had some project or nice paper on the bulletin board. I smiled endlessly and was prepared to answer a multitude of questions about my grading policies and classroom discipline plans. However, during my last year of classroom teaching, Open House Night changed the way I looked upon the effect I had upon my students. A young woman walked into my classroom with her son in tow. She brought him to me and said, "You listen to Mrs. Chamberlain. She'll make you learn." It took me a minute; then I recognized her. She had been one of my students in sixth grade about 15 years earlier. I was pleased that she recognized me for I was teaching in a different school district, and I was even more pleased that she thought I would help her son learn. Later, when I was alone, I reflected on Sonia and the time we spent together.

Sonia was labeled a slow learner; she not only had difficulty learning, but she did not relate well to other students. Her clothes were dirty and her hair was unkempt. Other students made fun of her and claimed that she smelled. To be truthful, she did. The year Sonia was in my class, I was pregnant and often her smell made me feel nauseous. Yet, there was something about Sonia that I liked. When I paid the slightest bit of attention to her, she smiled.

One day, I decided to take things into my own hands and went to talk to the school nurse. We made arrangements for her to shower in the locker room. I bought her a hairbrush and we spent time practicing new hairstyles. Several times during the year, I gave her clips for her new hairstyles. This is what I remember about Sonia. She remembers me as a teacher who helped her learn. What did I help her learn? Perhaps the more important question is what did she help me learn?

During the year Sonia's son was in my class, she tried to help him with his homework, even though it was difficult for her. She called me when she couldn't understand notes or letters that went home from school. Her son came to school regularly. She faithfully came to parent conferences. I can't claim that just because I spent time with Sonia, her life was changed but in my heart I have to believe that I might have played a small part in the development of her attitude about school and learning. I began to realize that teaching involved more than academics; our relationships with students may affect them forever.

My journey to become an advocate for middle level education and a student of adolescent development actually began in 1971 when I, a second-year teacher, started teaching sixth grade in a middle school beginning its second year of existence. I joined a four-person interdisciplinary team made up of experienced and beginning teachers. We experimented with team teaching, team meetings, X-mods (advisory periods?), creating our own group and class scheduling. We integrated curriculum—although we didn't refer to it as such. We tried to develop activities that would interest our students. The teachers and students became a "team" with our own group identity. Over the years our team of teachers separated because of administrative reassignments or life changes. Yet, my years as a middle school teacher remain on my list of professional career highlights. I continued friendships with some students who were on our team during the years we were together.

In the course of my professional career, I have taught preschool through undergraduate levels, served as an elementary school principal, and functioned as curriculum director for grades K-12. During the time I spent working with primary children, I became familiar with the term "developmentally appropriate." Nevertheless, I never lost my interest in the education of the young adolescent. I watched my two sons grow through adolescence. I began to wonder, if developmentally appropriate is important for schooling the young child, shouldn't it be just as important for the schooling of the young adolescent? My interest in child development and educational psychology blossomed.

Eventually, I chanced upon an article by Nel Noddings in which she challenged her readers to question their ways of thinking about schools (1995). This article led me to her book, *The Challenge to Care in Schools*. Her words, her ideas, began to tug at me. "[M]ost teachers work very hard and express deep concerns for their students. In an important sense, teachers do care, but they are unable to make the connections that would complete caring relationships with their students" (1992, 2). I asked myself, if teachers do care and are working in earnest, why aren't the connections being made?

When I decided to conduct an in-depth study of curriculum, there was no question as to what was important to me—middle schools and the students for whom they are designed. I found that discussions with former students often centered on activities and relationships developed at the middle school. Views of former students about their experiences piqued my interest. As my journey continued, the need to explore constructivist theory, community theory, and systems theory became apparent. I gained new insights into feminist theory, began to make connections between my beliefs and the tenets of these perspectives, and gained a greater respect for educational research.

As I delved deeper into the study of adolescents, I found that students bring multiple perspectives to their school experiences. I spent some time talking with middle school students about their perceptions of their learning environment. It was they who started discussions about gender equity and the impact of economic status on what was happening with them in school. Before I talked with the students, I suspected there may be gender issues; my reading of middle school literature told me as much. But then, I heard it from the students themselves. This was not just theory; this was reality in the lives of middle school students. Later, after I joined the education faculty at a small liberal arts college, I talked to the principal of a middle school where I wanted to place student teachers from our teacher education program. He bluntly told me that he really didn't want student teachers from our institution because he felt that our students didn't understand diversity issues that they would face in his school. Middle school students told me about gender and economic status; the principal told me about cultural differences. Clearly stakeholders in middle schools were identifying needs. I wondered what the future held for middle school education.

A Personal Perspective

As I explored the issues I faced, I realized that it was important to acknowledge my cultural background, assumptions, and values. In order to understand others, I had to understand myself. As a young adolescent, I did not grow up in a diverse community. The only real diversity I encountered was religious diversity. Some of my friends attended churches that celebrated different holidays with different traditions. I can remember being curious and in awe of the pageantry of their services and the special foods they served during holidays. I remember hearing their "Bubbas" talk in Slavic. But language wasn't an issue between my friends and me. Moreover, it was a small town and in order to have friends at all, one needed to be friends with everyone.

It was not until my high school years when we moved to a larger town that I encountered prejudice and segregation for the first time. I can remember being confused that my black friend could not go to the community swimming pool with me. Then I remember becoming angry. I remember learning that black families couldn't buy properties in certain areas of town. This angered me. I didn't notice just racial discrimination, however. Socio-economic status made a big difference in the school environment. Maybe it was because the school was large, but it seemed that there was definitely the "in-crowd" and the onlookers. All this in a nice, northern college town.

In college I was a "townie" and moved between two worlds, campus and home, but did not feel part of either. I went to the local college because I knew my two younger brothers wanted to go to college and money was tight; I was *just going to be a teacher* so the local college would be fine. In many ways, I did not know how the system worked. I took the courses I was told to take and observed campus life from the outside. I even did my student teaching in my hometown. When I questioned this placement, my advisor told me that they assigned me there as a favor because they knew I didn't have the money to live out of town.

Civil rights, race riots, Viet Nam, SDS, and the Black Panthers were in the forefront of the news. I knew about political activism and even boycotted grapes, yet I did not "get involved." I remember anxiously watching the draft lottery and breathing a sigh of relief because my brothers' numbers were high and they probably wouldn't be drafted. I believed in causes yet economics, family responsibilities, and my own insecurities drained my energy.

As a beginning teacher, I moved to a small town in the Northeast where I was a stranger. It didn't take me long however to see distinct social groups within the school. There certain "names" were linked to the "troublemakers." Where you lived in relationship to the one stoplight in town signified your status. I learned that it was not socially acceptable for someone for the north part of town to date someone from the south part of town. I noticed that certain physical characteristics were common in children from *that* part of town.

The segregation was based upon a mixture of economic and racial differences. I learned that children from the south part of town had an interesting heritage. Their families were descendants from some of the earliest settlers in the area, but through inter-racial marriages and reversals of fortune, they became the undesirables.

My middle school students knew that there was discrimination and prejudice. They told me so. The term "high society" was frequently used to describe students who lived north of the red light or who were in one of the higher socio-economic groups of the community. I remember one girl in particular commenting that all teachers were "high society" and lived north of the red light. When I told her that I lived south of the red light, she commented that I was OK.

Later, when I read about the practice of tracking in secondary schools and learned that a high percentage of minority students were in lower tracks, I thought of my former students. It was true. The south kids were mostly in the lower tracks. "Southies" had their own dialect, and other children were cautioned to be careful that they didn't talk "south talk." When children misbehaved, they were told to stop acting like a "Southie." Even when one went out dancing, others were quick to point out those who were doing the "south town shuffle." Clearly, the culture of those from south town was not valued. For some reason, the south students and I got along fairly well, as well as middle school teachers and students can get along, I guess. Perhaps in a way I was able to empathize with them.

I don't really remember discussing diversity issues in any of my undergraduate or master's degree work. The colleges had very white, middle-class student bodies and the professors were the same. Nevertheless, I became aware of gender issues in my program for my principal's certification. I took a course in curriculum theory and realized that all the experts quoted in the textbook were men. I remember writing a paper about women in administration and commenting that Maria Montessori wasn't even mentioned in the textbook used in the course. Most teachers I knew were women; most school administrators were men. When I became a principal, I became a member of a minority and experienced being an "other."

I completed my doctoral work at a large research institution. I encountered different, sometimes confusing, perspectives. At one point, I questioned my own ability and right to be in a doctoral program on such a campus. The language of academe was not mine; I did not know the words that I was reading or professors were using in class. My language of practice in the classroom was not the language of theory. I sat one memorable Sunday afternoon on my bed alone in a dorm room and sobbed. I questioned if I, a middle-aged educator from a rural area, belonged among the widely traveled, young, sophisticated graduate students. After I regained my composure, my resolve returned. I decided language was not going to be a barrier to my success. I developed a word box system, much like the one I used when teaching middle school reading, and every time I encountered a new word, I wrote it on an index card and added it to the box. I had to infer meanings, for many of the words weren't in the "collegiate" dictionary I purchased. I learned the words that enabled me to converse in the educational research world. I could have given up.

It was also in graduate school that I fully appreciated how the diversified student body and faculty enriched my life and my learning. I engaged in conversations that opened my eyes to ideas I had not even considered. I spent time with classmates from Kenya, Puerto Rico, Jamaica, and China. They talked about their experiences, and I talked about mine. It became very clear that students from different cultures have different expectations and views about education. At the same time, I was researching middle school theory and how students see their school experiences.

I learned that our population is diversifying much more than we are acknowledging in middle school literature. Some statisticians suggest that over the next twenty or so years, the number of students who are in what we term "minority" groups today will outnumber students of European descent. I have heard this trend termed as the "browning" of America. I realized that this is an oversimplification and does not really tell the whole story. Schools will experience increased diversity in language, religion, ethnicity, and even economic resources. I realized there is a need to consider middle school organization and pedagogy through multicultural perspectives. I wondered how middle schools will meet their challenges in a diverse society.

Multicultural Education

When I acknowledged that middle level schools needed to address diversity, I thought, "Aha. *Multicultural education* is the answer." But in my search for information, I found that there are different interpretations of multicultural education. According to Christine Sleeter and Carl A. Grant (1987), renowned experts in multicultural education, there is a wide range of multicultural education programs and philosophies. They call the first approach the *Teaching the Exceptional and Culturally Different Approach*. In this approach, the dominant culture is taught and the goal is to fit students into existing social structures. Teachers adapt regular teaching and remedial strategies based upon students' learning styles. Most often, this is a pull-out program. The underlying assumption is that the problem belongs to the students. Student ethnic and cultural groups are often generalized without acknowledging differences within groups.

The second approach is called the *Human Relations Approach*. The goal of this program is to encourage relationships and school harmony. Often there are lessons about stereotyping and individual differences. Although teachers are taught to honor diversity, in reality assimilation between cultures and genders is desired. Teaching strategies such as cooperative learning are used; however, there is often little connection between theory and practice.

Programs for Ethnic Studies or Women's Studies are examples of the third approach that Sleeter and Grant label the *Single Group Studies Approach*. The underlying assumption is that in the past biases existed therefore knowledge about special groups should be presented separately. The goal is to promote equality for recognized groups. The programs emphasize the history, culture, and contributions of the group. A shortcoming of this approach is that it does not address multiple forms of diversity.

The *Multicultural Approach* emphasizes cultural pluralism and is organized around different cultural groups. The literature focuses on racial and ethnic groups, although gender and social class differences may be included. Students are encouraged to employ thinking skills and analyze social situations. Contributions of many cultures are honored and multilingual acquisition is encouraged. Students are encouraged to maintain their native languages. Teachers are asked to look at their own teaching strategies.

The final approach extends previous approaches and is called *Education That Is Multicultural and Social Reconstructionist*. Major goals are to have students analyze social inequalities and oppression while developing skills for social action. Cultural pluralism and equality for all people are promoted. So it seems that those who are planning programs to address diversity must come to consensus about the approach they will use. As readers can by now probably infer, the final approach appeals to me.

Multicultural education, then, according to my perspective is not an add-on that teachers must incorporate into existing curriculum. Teachers do not "do multiculturalism" by adding the works of a few female or black or Asian authors to a literature list or by having pictures of minorities prominently displayed around the classroom or by making sure that the number of times the pronoun "she" is used equals the number of times "he" is used.

Multicultural education is not remediation; it does not fix deficiencies that some groups of students bring to the classroom. Multicultural education is a vehicle for social action and change. It does not prop up students to make them successful within an existing system; it analyzes the existing system and advocates change. Adolescents are interested in social issues (NMSA 1995); middle school education can support and promote change. Therefore, addressing diversity issues in an atmosphere of change is consistent with adolescent needs and development. I will expand on this concept in Chapter 2.

I believe that school programs designed to address the needs of their diverse students will acknowledge and build upon this diversity. This is indeed a challenge because educators as a whole do not constitute a diverse population. Nor are we sure of the cultures students will bring with them to the classroom. Thus, my understanding of a developmentally appropriate approach was modified through reflection and new knowledge. Not only will middle school educators deal with the physical, emotional/psychological, social, intellectual, and moral development of their students, but they will work with students whose experiences throughout adolescence are mitigated by their diversity. Through exploring the issues, I developed diversity themes that will be an important part of middle level education: gender, language, religion, race and ethnicity, and socio-economic status. Although these themes are listed separately, they are not independent of each other. They are intertwined in the lives of students and teachers.

Gender

When one mentions *gender studies* the reaction often includes references to "that feminist stuff" or veiled references to homosexuality. Gender studies include much more. When we consider gender, we are considering the roles that individuals fulfill as defined by society. Sex is biological; gender is determined by roles in society. We ascribe the label masculine or feminine to characteristics of individuals. According to societal expectations, girls are "supposed" to act in a certain way and boys are "supposed" to act in a certain way. David and Myra Sadker in their seminal book *Failing at Fairness: How America's Schools Cheat Girls* (1994), tell us that girls are treated differently than boys in school. Williams Pollack, in his books, *Real Boys* (1998) and *Real Boys*

Voices (2000), tells us that boys who don't fit society's macho image of masculinity are penalized. Clearly, school practices affecting boys and girls require investigation.

We cannot confine the issue of gender to the visible biological divisions of boys and girls. Each individual has masculine and feminine characteristics that vary in degree. Studies suggest that up to 10% of teenagers in schools today identify themselves as gay or lesbian. If that percentage is applied to a classroom of 30 students we are talking about 3 students–3 students who may feel different or disenfranchised by classroom practices. When classroom practices do not address the individuality, students suffer.

For many years, Kohlberg's stages of moral development were accepted as the norm until Carol Gilligan challenged his theory. His theory was based upon research with boys; Gilligan suggested that a feminine perspective may shed a different light upon the theory. She found that girls tend to be more concerned with relationships issues when making moral decisions than boys (Gilligan 1982). Differences between the physical development of boys and girls are accepted. Yet, acknowledgment of differences in other areas of development lags behind. Social, cognitive, and emotional developmental differences between boys and girls are becoming more apparent as evidence by the work of Gilligan, Pollack, and others. More and more, the need to consider both masculine and feminine perspectives appears when we look at all aspects of school life, including curriculum and social interaction.

Language Diversity

A second area of diversity is language diversity. My aunts tell me that when they were children, they were not allowed to learn German, the native language of their grandparents. The children were to only speak English, even though occasionally, when the adults didn't want little ones to understand, adults spoke German. This was the way it was for many immigrants who wanted to assimilate into the American way of life. Speaking English was the key to social and economic advancement in their eyes.

Children of immigrant families today are faced with language difficulties. We cannot assume that the preferred language at home is English, although for some it may be. We cannot generalize about the needs of students or parents for whom English is the second language. Nor can we assume that all Native Americans speak "Indian" or all those from Mexico speak the same Spanish.

Among groups we may find a multitude of dialects that result from geographic or even economic differences. We will need to learn about students as individuals to understand their perspectives.

We can't confine our discussion about linguistically diverse students to immigrant children. In our increasingly mobile society, families move from one section of the country to another. Colloquial words and phrases may cause problems for students. But it is not just the geographically mobile children who are face with language differences. To be upwardly mobile socially and economically, it is often necessary to be able to conversing in certain manners; "factory talk" and "management talk" sound different. Students' academic achievement is often judged upon their fluency with standard English.

I once worked with a student who was infamous for her "barn talk." She could make a grown man blush in school. The barn talk was the language she heard and used at home. Nevertheless, this same language set her apart from most of the students in her class. I had to help her learn that, although the language she used was acceptable in her home environment, it was not appropriate for school. I did not want to dishonor her family. I could not let her believe I thought her parents were "bad" because of their language. We had to negotiate the school–home difference.

Religious Diversity

As a principal, I encountered the resentment of some teachers and parents when I insisted on changing the "Christmas Concert" to a "Winter Concert" in consideration of those who could not participate on religious grounds. Even other members of our administrative team did not support the change. To me, this seemed such a minor change; I was just changing words. In this case however, the words symbolized tradition and were emotionally connected. Nevertheless, religious diversity goes beyond the outer trappings of school activities. Religion is a difference that may guide decisions based upon beliefs and values. Sometimes the only outward manifestation of diversity is dress or actions.

Early in my career as a classroom teacher, I had students who belonged to a religious group that had norms that were quite different from those of the other students in the classroom. In this group, girls always wore dresses, members didn't celebrate holidays, and they didn't participate in the Pledge of Allegiance. I wanted to make these students feel comfortable, yet their beliefs put them at odds with many classroom practices. I had to consider how our customary activities excluded some students from participation. But in addition, I had to consider how these students felt and how other students reacted to their differences.

Since September of 2001, religious differences have had an increasing impact upon our perceptions of others. We as a global community have had to try to untangle the political and religious involvement in world events such as terrorism. Unfortunately, lack of knowledge has proven to be an obstacle. Muslim students who are citizens of the United States are targets of hate and reprisal because of their religion. Differences among Islamic traditions are not considered. Anger and fear color relationships. Teachers are challenged to address their own emotions while creating supportive learning environments and classroom practices.

Racial and Ethnic Diversity

A more visible diversity among students is race. We usually identify members of a race by their physical characteristics. Yet, according to some, there is no biological basis for race; they suggest that individuals exhibit characteristics that are variants of genetic material. Race is a socially constructed concept. For instance, the Irish were considered an inferior race by the English, yet were able to assume their whiteness gradually in American society. Other immigrant groups had similar experiences at one time or another in our nation's history. Now, it appears that skin color is a convenient way to define race and a very visible one. We have great diversity among our students based upon physical attributes and the way the students see themselves in the context of race. Often connected with race is the concept of racism, the domination of one group by another based upon race; our American society has a legacy of racism.

Until the landmark United States Supreme Court case of *Loving v. Virginia* in 1967, biracial marriage, especially between blacks and whites, was illegal in many states. Since that time, the number of biracial couples has grown dramatically and correspondingly, the number of biracial children in school has grown. Today, biracial persons are more prominent than when I was a teenager. Teens have role models like Mariah Carey and Tiger Woods. However, support for biracial and multiracial children is still lacking in schools. I found literature for and about biracial and multiracial children is scarce, for example.

Another issue often associated with race is the concept of ethnicity. An ethnic group is one in which members share common beliefs and values. The members show membership in the group by outward signs such as common language, religion, foods, or music. Members may choose to identify with an ethnic group. Early in our history, in an effort to conform to the melting pot ideal of American society, many members of ethnic groups tried to hide their ethnicity. Recently, however, pride in one's ethnicity has been acceptable and even encouraged. *Ethnocentrism*, considering one's own ethnic group superior to others, strains efforts to support diversity. Historically, contributions of minority ethnic groups have been devalued. In a diverse school community, we will be challenged to respect differences among our students and to honor the contributions that enrich our school environment.

Social and Economic Diversity

As I reflect upon typical years as a middle school teacher, I realize that money or the lack of it dictated student participation in school life. There were yearbook sales, pretzel sales, book orders, and ski club trips. Book orders, for instance, are a common occurrence in an elementary or middle school classroom. The teacher passes out attractive book order forms and then collects money from students and sends in the order. Class time is often used in the process. Then when the order arrives, the books are ceremoniously distributed. There are students who order multiple books every time and receive prized "bonus books" or the teacher receives "bonus points" which he or she can redeem for books, cameras, or even microwave ovens based upon the volume or value of the order. However, there are students who don't order books. Some sit quietly while classmates excitedly show their bounty; some feign indifference; others declare that they don't like to read and really didn't want to order any books. But the pressure is there. I remember one young boy who actually stole money from a classmate's desk in order to place an order. He was wrong and I certainly do not excuse his behavior. But I can understand. He succumbed to the pressure.

Economics also plays a role in academic participation. I did not grow up in an affluent family by any stretch of the imagination, but our house always had books, magazines, and newspapers. Early in my career, in my naiveté I assumed that every house had them. I gave homework assignments that required students to use dictionaries and bring in newspaper clippings and then chided students for not doing their homework. I wasn't aware of socio-economic factors that impact on students. During my career I had had students who had no floors in their homes, who had no heat, or had no running water. Others did not know where they would sleep each night; they stayed with friends or relatives or stayed in homeless shelters. They had so many issues, and academics were not always a priority in their lives. Socio-economic status is usually determined by income, educational attainment, or occupation of the parents; the children may carry the burden of this status in school.

Children, according to some estimates, make up over half the chronic poor and 1 in 4 children may be considered poor. Again, if we think about an average classroom, we may be talking about 4 to 8 children in each group. Even more troublesome is the fact that 1 in 7 children have no health insurance (US Department of Commerce 1998). Young adolescents, who are growing rapidly and need nutritional meals and healthcare, do not have access to basic needs. As curriculum director, I tracked student numbers for free and reduced lunches in our district. Some children in the district received both breakfast and lunch at school. In some of our elementary buildings as many as 57% of the students qualified for federal lunch programs, yet when students moved on to the middle or high school the number of students applying for the program dropped to 18%. This may suggest that some adolescents do not want the stigma of being a "free luncher" so they go without eating.

Socio-economic status does not only affect students' lives in school. Many families are able to provide their children with additional opportunities that indirectly affect school performance. These students have the advantage of travel; art, music or theater; or even elaborate educational toys. In this age of technology, students with Internet access have resources beyond what we even imagined when I was a beginning teacher. Advantaged students may bring knowledge gained in these activities with them and are able to make connections with new material presented in the classroom.

Even though I am concentrating on middle level education, I must share an experience I had with a kindergarten student. She was having great difficulty in her reading readiness activities in a unit about beaches and turtles. Upon investigation, we realized that she did not know what these were. She had no experiences, no background knowledge, with which to connect new ideas. When we had a conference with her mother, we asked if the little girl watched Sesame Street. Her mother didn't know what Sesame Street was; this occurred in an environment where the program had been part of children's lives for over 25 years. Big Bird and Cookie Monster are part of the dominant culture. The concept of *cultural capital* holds that young people who are exposed to informal knowledge about how to dress, how to talk, or how to act have advantages over those who do not. Students with cultural capital know how to behave in social situations; they know how to deal with others in socially accepted ways; they know the language for success and the "rules" for acceptance. The kindergarten child lacked the cultural capital to be successful in her classroom.

Parents who have professional careers tend to become involved in their children's schools. Many working-class parents do not, but it is not because they are not interested in the children. Work schedules of these parents may conflict with scheduled conference times or parents may not feel they have the knowledge to be involved. They may feel inferior to teachers and other parents in the school. While I was director of federal programs in our district, we invited some parents to attend a workshop especially designed for them. One mother whom we invited at first said she did not want to go. When we talked to her, we found that she did not want to go because she felt she did not have the proper clothes to wear. The workshop was going to be held at a local conference center that usually catered to business travelers. We thought this location would be a "treat" for the parents; instead it was a deterrent.

Challenging Assumptions

Like so many others, I spent many years believing I am not biased or prejudiced. I was not challenged to examine my own assumptions. I realize now that we are all products of our experiences. I did not look upon myself as a member of an ethnic group, race, or economic level that has privileges in our society. I was not even cognizant of limitations that I may have experienced, because of my gender or "cultural capital." I cannot claim to have experienced what others experience or know what others know. I can only attempt to respect, care, and have empathy for others.

Through my reflections, I realized that diversity issues have played an important part of my development as an educator. The next step for me was to discover what kind of school environment support student diversity. The Carnegie Council (1989) recommends that a middle school be a learning community. The task of creating a community of learners suggests this question: What is a community of learners?

I suggest that such a community encourages teachers and students to engage in dialogue to create opportunities for learning and encourage them to listen to each other in order to understand each other's positions and shared meanings. We each have multiple identities. I am a white, middle-aged woman, a wife, a mother, a professional—I could go on. Each of us has a story about how we have come to where we are in our beliefs, values, and assumptions. It is tempting to try to categorize students by essentialized diversities. Nevertheless, each of our students has multiple identities and through these multiple identities interacts within the school community.

In the next chapter, I will review my understandings of middle school policy and philosophy as presented by three major organizations, the Carnegie Council on Adolescent Development, the National Association of Secondary School Principals, and the National Middle School Association. These representative organizations work at state and national levels to improve middle level education and to bring the needs of young adolescents to public attention. Over and over again, writers cite work published by these organizations. In my studies, I identified common themes within documents published by these organizations. I have labeled these themes "challenges for middle level organizations."

CHAPTER 2

Developmental Responsiveness

During my educational journey, I encountered theories about middle schools, adolescent development and learning environments. Many of these evolved as I was evolving; some emerged after I began teaching. I grew as an educator as middle schools were growing. As I learned about theories of adolescence, I realized that some of my intuitions about adolescents were validated; however, some of my assumptions were challenged. I struggled to have classroom environments that supported my students at the same time research about learning environments was beginning. This chapter traces the history of middle level education and discusses theories of adolescent development that influence middle level theories. It also introduces the concept of middle level schools as learning communities.

Historical Perspectives

Historical perspectives helped me to understand power structures that influenced the development of middle schools during the twentieth century. In the early 1900s, G. Stanley Hall began using the term *adolescent* and suggested that the adolescent years were characterized by turmoil. About the same time, social and economic forces in the United States prompted organization of schools for young adolescents, namely junior high schools. These schools were preparatory for high schools and often modeled after high school organization and curriculum. Middle level education responded to political and economic factors in the beginning half of the twentieth century. As the number of immigrant children swelled the classroom rolls and young adolescents left school to enter the labor market, middle level schools were called upon to assimilate immigrants into the dominant culture and the keep children in school and out of the workforce.

In the middle of the twentieth century, educators called for schools specifically designed for young adolescents based upon developmental needs. Even though the ideal of especially designed instruction for young adolescents was touted, in reality many middle schools were established purely for economic reasons. The baby boom generation's impact upon school enrollment caused crowded classrooms and school boards were faced with decisions about how to house students. Middle schools seemed to provide the solution by moving fifth and sixth graders from the crowded elementary buildings and moving seventh and eighth grade students from the high school buildings. These new organizational levels were no longer junior high schools for fifth and sixth graders were included. Thus, in the 1960s middle schools began to appear. Those who embraced the middle school concept were pleased; those who controlled finances were pleased. My experience was consistent with the trend. The middle school where I taught was based upon the middle school concept and at the same time addressed the economic needs of the district and relieved crowded elementary and high school conditions. We were off to a good start.

Current Conditions

Population is shrinking in the community where I began teaching. The middle school that housed over 1,000 students in the 1970s now has an enrollment of about 500. The middle school concept is being discarded; the new construction and renovation plan is for a consolidated elementary building and a junior/senior high building. It appears that the special needs of young adolescents did not prevail; taxpayers looked for an economical way to realign the district. Thus, a school district that founded a middle school in the 1970s and was a pioneer in meeting adolescent needs, yielded to the power of economics.

Yet, other communities are investigating the middle school concept for the first time. Not too far away from the district where I began teaching, a district has embraced the middle school concept. They have spent several years planning for the needs of young adolescents. Their new direction includes planning and renovation for a building especially designed to support the middle school concept. I wonder if districts that support the development of such schools are responding to economic pressures or are they indeed concerned about the needs of early adolescents. Perhaps it can be both.

Middle level school philosophy, in an attempt to bridge the gap between the self-contained elementary classrooms and the discipline-oriented secondary schools, recommends a blend of teachers with both professional backgrounds. This pedagogically is a logical proposal; however, economics and professional status have damaged the professional image of middle level teachers. Historically, elementary teachers, who were usually women, were considered to be less professionally qualified and could be hired cheaply. Women were considered appropriate teachers to nurture young children but were not believed capable to teach the *difficult content* in the high schools. Secondary teachers who did not quite meet the standard expected of high school teachers were often "demoted" to the middle level schools. Thus, an inferior image of middle level teaching emerged. Today, middle level education is often considered to be a way station for administrators or teachers who want to be promoted to the high school. Even as my state legislature acknowledged the need for specialized training for middle level teachers, a local school board decreed that anyone hired to teach in seventh or eighth grade in their middle school in the future would need secondary school teaching certification. They believed that elementary teachers did not have the ability to teach the difficult content for middle school. They negated the knowledge of child development that many elementary teachers bring to the classroom. The state now agrees. I have a friend who has a Ph.D. and specialized in science education who will no longer be able to teach her 7th grade science classes because she has elementary certification. These regulations negate the knowledge of child development that many elementary teachers bring to the classroom and assume that elementary certified teachers do not have content knowledge. Old ideas and assumptions prevail. Interestingly, some research suggests that eighth grade students show greater achievement when they are in programs that are aligned with elementary school principles (Renchler 2000).

Middle level schools have reacted to the ebb and flow of the forces within society. Schools at all levels reacted to the progressive education movement, to the Cold War and the impact of Sputnik, to the Civil Rights movement, and even now to the call for national standards. Through all these times, teachers and students have attempted to negotiate the balance between the needs of society and lives of students. Often, when I talk to others about my interest in middle schools and young adolescents, they look at me and shake their heads. They quickly admit that middle school teaching would not be their preference. What frightens educators about middle schools and young adolescents? Middle school education is proposed to meet the developmental needs of early adolescents. Before considering whether schools meet their challenges, we need to consider the meaning of "developmentally appropriate." What distinguishes the middle level learner from students in other age groups?

Developmental Theories

Developmental theories suggest distinct characteristics of the early adolescent that range from those related to psychoanalytic theories, such as outlined by Erik Erikson, to social cognition theories as proposed by Robert Selman. Generally, theorists agree that the period from around the age of 10 to the age of 14 is a time of transition and the onset of puberty is a defining variable. Debates do occur, however, about the role of biology and socio-cultural influences on the way these characteristics develop.

Psychoanalytic theories base most of the descriptions of the early adolescent period on the work of Freud. Freud suggested that the young adolescent is moving from the period of sexual latency to puberty at the end of the elementary school years. During the latency period, a child identifies with parents and develops important social, moral, and cultural values. At the end of the latency period, same-sex friendships become strong, often to the exclusion of friends of the opposite sex. The onset of puberty indicates the beginning of adolescence and is marked by increasing sexual tension that is mediated by social, moral, and cultural conditions. This tension reaches its peak at about the age of 15 (Mitchell and Black 1995). According to Freudian theories, adolescents should not be frustrated by repressive, prudish restraints; instead an atmosphere that creates feelings of security and love is appropriate; and all behavior can be traced to underlying causes. Young adolescents behave the way they do for a reason. When they are defiant, are they lacking in love or security?

Erik Erikson (1963/1998), a student of Freud, suggested that personal development is contingent on an individual's progression from one developmental crisis to another and that each crisis must be achieved before an individual can progress to the next. According to his theory, the average young adolescent is moving from the period of *Industry v. Inferiority* into the period of

Identity v. Role Confusion. The first of these two stages usually occurs during the ages of 6 to 12 and is marked by students acquiring the basic knowledge and skills for participation in society. During this period children learn to take pride in their work. If the crisis of Industry, of success, is successfully met, student feelings about self will be positive. During the period of Identity v. Role Confusion, usually from ages 12 to 18, students adjust to their rapidly changing bodies and deal with social pressures about their present and future directions. This period is marked with an increased emphasis on peer group relationships as students attempt to explore and test roles. According to Erikson, the period of early adolescence is especially turbulent, as during this period the young person must struggle with rapid changes while dealing with a sense of psychological crises around the development of an identity.

James Marcia built on Erikson's work when he proposed that there are four statuses in identity development for adolescents. He identified one as *identity achievement* that occurs when adolescents have explored their identities and made choices. He stated that few adolescents achieve this status until late high school or after. The *identity foreclosure* status, according to Marcia, is the result of adolescents not exploring options and making choices based on the wishes of others, particularly their parents. Another status, *diffusion*, occurs when adolescents have not explored their options or perhaps never considered their options and thus are confused about their choices or direction. The *moratorium* status is a period of exploration and is common in today's young adolescents. During this period youth are actively involved in exploring their identities (Woolfolk 1998). This status is consistent with middle school philosophy that holds that young adolescents are curious and eager to explore.

Peter Blos's interpretation of psychoanalytical theory stressed the separation from parental influences. During the adolescent period, a young person may regress to early stages as the negotiation of new roles emerges. Unlike Freud, Blos suggested that the period of preadolescence involves the development of sexual tendencies and young adolescents are concerned with body changes and image. An important contribution of Blos was the interjection of the necessity to consider feminine perspectives and differences in development (Blos 1962; Muus 1982).

Cultural anthropologists, encouraged by the work of Margaret Mead, suggest that the young person's adjustment to puberty is culturally and socially mediated; our Western culture exacerbates adolescent turmoil. According to such theories, the vast differences apparent in the early adolescents in Western culture are caused by the heterogeneity of cultures, the rapidity of cultural changes, and the diversified cultural and hereditary background of the young people. Secular trend, the tendency for members of each generation to reach puberty earlier than those of the previous one, combined with the earlier mimicking of adult life styles, contributes to the increased anxieties experienced among early adolescents. These problems are most acute during the high school years according to Mead (Ausubel 1968; Muus 1982).

Havighurst stressed developmental tasks that are acquired through physical maturity, social expectations, and personal effort. He introduced the key concept of a "teachable moment"—an opportune time to teach a task. He suggested that developmental tasks different from culture to culture, therefore students may face specific tasks at different points in their lives (Havighurst 1952; Rice 1999).

Kurt Lewin (1951) proposed the theory that behavior is a function of the interaction of the person with an environment, commonly known as "field theory." This interaction, or life space, for an adolescent is influenced by both biological and social factors. The structure of the life space decreases and freedom to move within the life space increases as one moves from childhood to adolescence. As the young adolescent moves into previously unavailable spaces, conflict and uncertainty can occur. Young people, as they explore, get mixed messages from adults who at one time treat them like children and at another time treat them as adults. An added stress in the transitional period for adolescents, according to field theory, is the impact of individual and cultural differences (Muus 1982).

Selman proposed a theory of social cognition that is based upon development of abilities to understand and know others. He suggested that intellectual ability and social ability do not necessarily develop at the same rate. Interpersonal relationships are important (Muus 1982; Rice 1999). This theory reminds me of Daniel Goleman's book, *Emotional Intelligence* (1999), in which he suggests that schools can have an important role in developing this facet of students' personalities.

In contrast to field theory and social cognition theory, Arnold Gessell proposed a maturational theory suggesting that growth cannot be prompted by external factors and that time alone will permit development according to Ames, Ilg, and Baker, devotees of Gessell's work. In their book, *Your Ten-to-Fourteen-Year Old* (1952), they propose that the ages 10 to 14 can be described distinctly. They suggest that the age of 10 is a period of equilibrium during which the child is comfortable with himself or herself and others. The 11-year-old child, however is quite different. This is a time of discord and a time for students to test the limits of authority. On the other hand, 12-year-olds tend to be tolerant and enthusiastic. The 13-year old, in contrast, is often withdrawn, self-conscious, and moody. Fourteen-year olds love the new and different and have boundless energy. Ames, Ilg, and Baker caution, however, that understanding any one child requires consideration of the child's basic understandings, appreciation of the child's developmental level, and the child's environment (1952)

As I tried to make sense of these and many other theories, I found that each theory gave me a piece of the information I was seeking, yet none of them completely fit my assumptions or interpretations of my experiences. Table 2.1 shows how I made sense of some theories that seemed to relate to middle school issues. I also realized that a theory is someone else's explanation of what he or she observes. Most of the perspectives of adolescent development that are found in educational literature were developed by white, Euro-American males. Notable exceptions are theories of Margaret Mead (1961/1973) and Carol Gilligan (1982). They did present a perspective from Euro-American culture, however.

Each of the theories I studied added to my understandings, yet they raised questions. I wondered how our accepted practices in middle level education were in concert with developmental theories. For instance, Erikson's theory (1963/1998) made me question if we provide opportunities for students to experience success, to achieve the crisis of Industry. Margaret Mead's proposition about secular trend (Ausubel 1968; Muus 1982) makes me wonder if indeed middle school students of the twenty-first century will be more mature than the students I taught in the early 1970s. Furthermore, throughout all my research about adolescent development I could not help but notice that the key concepts of relationships with others and supportive learning environment seemed to be appearing.

In subsequent chapters I will refer to theories as they apply to practices within middle schools, but I will also remember that there will be differences in approaches and interpretations. In this chapter I have only summarized the theories, for it is my hope that each reader will investigate the theories as they apply to unique situations and make sense of them in individual ways.

Table 2.1 Theories of Adolescence

FREUD—Psychoanalytic

- Unconscious of hidden drives influence emotions or behavior.
- Young adolescent is moving from a period of sexual latency to puberty that brings on adolescence. Period is marked by sexual tension and mediated by social, moral, and cultural conditions. (Mitchell and Black 1995)

BLOS—Psychoanalytic

- Adolescence is crucial to development.
- Adolescence is psychological and an individual's response to sexual and biological changes. Emotional separation from parents is crucial. Period has emphasis on the difference between male and female development. (Blos 1962; Muus 1982)

ERIKSON—Psychosocial

- Personal development is contingent upon an individual's progression from one developmental crisis to another and that each crisis must be achieved before an individual can progress to the next.
- Adolescence is especially turbulent; during this period the young person must struggle with rapid changes while dealing with a psychological crisis around the development of identity. (Erikson 1963/1998)

MEAD—Cultural Anthropology

- Emphasizes the importance of social environment interacting with biology in development.
- Young person's adjustment to puberty is culturally and socially mediated, and our Western culture exacerbates adolescent turmoil. Differences occur due to cultural and heredity backgrounds. (Ausubel 1968; Mead 1961/1973; Muus 1982)

LEWIN—Field Theory

- Behavior is function of the interaction of a person with the environment—life space.
- Adolescence is influenced by both biological and social factors; conflict and uncertainty can occur in adolescence as young people explore their life spaces. (Lewin 1951; Muus 1982)

Continued on next page

Table 2.1 continued

GESSELL—Maturation or Stage Theory

- Growth cannot be prompted by external factors; time alone will permit development.
- Age 10 is a time when the child is comfortable with himself or herself; 11 is a time of discord and testing authority; 12-year-olds are tolerant and enthusiastic; 13-year-olds are often withdrawn, self-conscious, and moody; 14-year-olds love the new and different and have boundless energy. (Ames, Ilg, and Baker 1952)

SELMAN—Social Cognition

- Knowing about others, their thoughts and feelings, is essential for getting along.
- During adolescence, young people begin to be able to take the perspectives of others and social perspectives; acknowledge that laws and moralities are social systems. (Muus 1982; Rice 1999)

HAVIGHURST—Psychosocial

- Developmental tasks vary from culture to culture depending on the importance of biological, psychological, and cultural elements in determining tasks. Some tasks are biological; others are social.
- Major tasks include: accepting physical self achieving; relationships with peers; achieving masculine or feminine sex roles; achieving emotional independence from parents; preparing for a career; preparing for marriage and family; developing socially responsible behavior; and acquiring values and ethical systems. (Havighurst 1952; Rice 1999)

KOHLBERG—Moral Development

- There are major levels of moral development. Progression from one level to another results from interactions with people from a higher stage.
- Between the ages of 9 and 20 is the stage when mores of society are followed unquestionably: 1—what will please or impress others; 2—what is right maintains social order. (Kohlberg 1981)

GILLIGAN—Moral Development

- Interpretation of Kohlberg's stages is biased against the female perspective
- Care and relationships are important in making choices according to the feminist perspective. (Gilligan 1982)

Developmentally Responsive Middle Schools

Literature about middle level education abounds; however, policy statements and literature published by three major organizations, the Carnegie Council on Adolescent Development (1989), the National Association of Secondary School Principals (NASSP) (1989; 1993), and the National Middle School Association (NMSA) (1995) appear to summarize current educational thought. Together, the three organizations have stated that the distinct purpose of middle level education is to meet the needs of the young adolescent. Each organization has described these needs and approached the implementation of such a mission based upon research conducted within their organizations and research literature about psychology, philosophy, and practice within schools.

Noted middle level education theorists such as Donald Eichhorn, William Alexander, and James Beane are listed among authors of NASSP and NMSA materials. The characteristics of young adolescents found in the varied theories of adolescent development seem to be summarized by the National Middle School Association in their position paper, *This We Believe: Developmentally Responsive Middle Level Schools* (1995). The NMSA cautions educators that these characteristics are group characteristics and individual differences will occur. The five areas of development identified include intellectual, moral, physical, emotional/psychological, and social development.

The National Middle School Association was founded in 1973 as an outgrowth of work begun in the 1960s by a working group of the Association for Supervision and Curriculum Development (ASCD) and the Midwest Middle School Association that was formed in 1970. By 1973, the Midwest group grew and became the National Middle School Association (Brough 1995). The NMSA organization "is dedicated to improving the education experiences of young adolescents by providing vision, knowledge, and resources to all who serve them in order to develop healthy, productive, and ethical citizens" (NMSA 1995, inside cover). According to the NMSA, effective middle schools have educators committed to young adolescents, are guided by a shared vision, have high expectations for all, have an adult advocate for every student, make family and community partnerships, and have a positive school climate.

The Council on Middle Level Education, a division of the National Association of Secondary School Principals, was established in 1981

> to help educators and citizens focus more clearly on the needs of young adolescents
> during the middle school years. These efforts have sought to refine the middle level

educational identity and generate materials to help school programs better respond to young adolescent educational needs. (National Association of Secondary School Principals [NASSP] 1989, p. v).

After the publication of *A Nation at Risk* in 1983, the NASSP Council on Middle Level Education published a series of *Agenda for Excellence* monographs. Within these monographs, the basic functions of middle schools were outlined. These tasks are considered to be reference points upon which the effectiveness of schools in their attempts to respond to student developmental needs could be measured. The functions include integration, exploration, guidance, socialization, articulation, and differentiations (NASSP 1989).

The Carnegie Council on Adolescent Development was sponsored by the Carnegie Corporation of New York in 1986 to provide non-educational perspectives about adolescents. The Carnegie Council on Adolescent Development prepared a seminal report, *Turning Points: Preparing American Youth for the 21st Century* in 1989 that included among its signatories Jacqueline Eccles, a noted educational researcher, and then-governor Bill Clinton. The council provided follow-up funding as grants to states interested in improving the education of young adolescents (Brough 1995; James 1995). *Turning Points* is widely accepted by those involved in middle level education and outlines goals and expectations for middle schools (Mills 1995; Reed and Russell 1995). Qualities of effective middle schools presented in the report included creating a learning community, teaching a core of common knowledge, insuring success for all students, and empowering teachers and administrators. According to the Carnegie Council, a student who has received an appropriate middle level education will be (1) an intellectually reflective person; (2) a person en route to a lifetime of meaningful work; (3) a good citizen; (4) a caring and ethical person; and (5) a healthy person. These goals and expectations for middle level education by a non-educational organization are similar to those proposed by other organizations such as the National Association of Secondary School Principals and the National Middle School Association. In 1998, the Carnegie Council published an updated version of their report, *Great Transitions: Preparing Adolescents for a New Century.*

Each organization proposes that middle level schools are vital in meeting the needs of young adolescents. The Carnegie Council on Adolescent Development suggests that middle level schools are the "most powerful source to recapture millions of youth adrift, and help every young person thrive through early adolescence" (1989, 10). The NASSP suggests that middle level schools address the needs of young adolescents as they move from elementary to secondary schools (1989). The NMSA emphasizes the developmental needs of early adolescents in their 1995 position paper. Integral in the literature from all these organizations is the concept of developmentally appropriate education for 10-to 15-year-old students.

Organizations cited in this chapter remind educators that young adolescents must be viewed holistically; i.e., their physical, intellectual, and social/emotional development and needs impact on their school experiences. Recommendations included in publications by the Carnegie Council, NASSP, and NMSA are based on consideration of developmental needs. Judith Brough (1990) states that the purpose of the middle school, and all educational institutions, is to promote healthy physical, social, emotional, and cognitive growth. Maynard (1986) reminds middle level educators about the diversity which students exhibit in these areas. Moreover, the varied psychological theories about the needs and characteristics of young adolescence suggest that working with young adolescents may not be an easy task. Therefore, these views and the qualities of developmentally responsive middle schools derived from the middle level education positions presented previously have been translated for the purpose of this work into five challenges to be addressed in middle level education: (1) to support students in the development of their identities; (2) to provide opportunities for success; (3) to encourage students in the development of relationships between peers and adults; and (4) to provide opportunities for students to practice citizenship which are all linked by (5) the challenge of flexibility (see Table 2.2). These challenges for middle level education address group needs, and at the same time deal with individual diversity—all within the context of the learning environment. The learning environment which students experience most directly is the classroom, and the individual teacher's attitudes and assumptions affect this particular learning environment.

The Learning Environment

Diversity found among the students in middle level schools presents challenges to educators who interact with students on a daily basis. Furthermore, Nel Noddings (1992) suggests that understanding and caring about oneself is fundamental to fostering positive relationships, respecting ideas and opinions of others, and achieving success. It is the adults within the school environment who have been challenged to address students' needs in a developmentally responsive way, certainly not an easy task. However, an appreciation of student diversity forms a foundation for the building of a learning community that provides experiences that promote the development of students' individual identities as learners. I believe that emphasis on student diversity is lacking in mainstream middle school literature, and my belief that multicultural education must be for social action colors my perceptions of the meaning of learning community.

Table 2.2   Challenges for Middle Level Education

CHALLENGE	DESCRIPTION
Identity Development	To provide learning experiences that promote the development of a student's individual identities as a learner, member of the family, school or community, and as a friend
Success	To provide opportunities for students to define, work toward, and experience success in developmentally appropriate skills and knowledge
Relationships	To provide opportunities for students to interact with peers and adults showing care, respect, and trust
Citizenship	To provide opportunities for students to be active participants in decisions about their learning activities and to address social issues by understanding the consequences of behaviors, by problem solving, and by being active participants in the learning community
Flexibility	To establish a learning environment, which through organizational structures—scheduling, facility usage, teaching methods, assessment and evaluation methods, courses, activities—addresses individual student's abilities, interest, and needs

The study of learning environment or classroom climate emerged about 30 years ago. Rudolph Moos (1976) proposed a social ecological approach that attempts to understand the environment from the perspective of the individual. This approach examines the environment and the ways individuals adapt, adjust, or cope with environments that can be stressful, limiting, selecting, releasing, or challenging. Embedded in his theories are ways environments can be organized in order to help individuals maximize their functioning and personal growth. This approach also is concerned with the control individuals have upon the environment and their freedom of choice. He concluded that environments, like people, have personalities that influence the people functioning within the environments. He suggests that an environment can be described by its emphasis on three dimensions.

The *Relationship* dimension includes the extent students are involved and participate in the classroom, how they related to others in the classroom, and the interaction between teachers and students. *The Personal Development* dimension includes those aspects that are related to task orientation and competitiveness for grades and recognition. The *System Maintenance and Change* dimension includes aspects that emphasize student behavior, rules clarity, student contributions to classroom activities, and the extent to which teachers use innovative techniques. Moos proposes that these dimensions have been linked to morale, self-confidence, academic performance, and school behavior (Moos 1976).

If we look at each of these dimensions, connections can be made between the dimensions and the challenges I propose for middle level education (see Figure 2.1). The first dimension, Relationship, identifies "the nature and intensity of personal relationships within the environment" (Moos 1976, 330). This relationship is concerned with the extent to which those involved within the environment support and help each other and with the extent to which there is spontaneity and free and open expression between the participants within the environment. If we look at the Citizenship and Relationship Challenges, clear connections appear. Relationships and the ability to take an active role in the school community fit within the parameters of middle school philosophy.

The Personal Development dimension, according to Moos, assesses the direction that "personal growth and self-enhancement tend to occur in the particular environment" (1976, 331). This dimension is related to the challenges of Success and Identity. As I propose, success means that students achieve developmentally appropriate skills and knowledge; the development of Identity includes personal growth.

The third dimension, System Maintenance and Change, evaluates "orderliness, the clarity of expectations, the degree of control, and the responsiveness to change" within the environment (Moos 1976, 331). This is related to the challenges of Flexibility and Citizenship. Without a doubt, flexibility includes responsiveness to change, participation, and sources of control within classrooms and the school.

Communities of Learning

The Carnegie Council recommends that a developmentally responsive middle school be a "community for learning" (1989, 37). The National Middle School Association supports the concept of a school climate that "promotes a sense of community and encourages learning" (1995, 18) and proposes that all stakeholders should be involved in a shared vision. The task of creating a community of learners suggests these questions: What is a community of learners? How does this relate to middle school education?

Figure 2.1   Relationship Between Moos's Dimensions and Challenges for Middle Level Schools

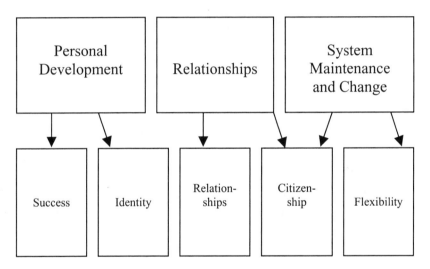

As I began reading about school communities, I found that Thomas Sergiovanni (1994) suggests that in a community of learners, students, teachers, and administrators engage in dialogue to create opportunities for learning, and knowledge is created by cooperation not competition. According to King and Brownell, a community is a "working, flourishing establishment, hence it is in a state of continual change, sometimes dynamic, sometimes nearly static. New rooms are added, others refurbished, some abandoned. Constant repair and upkeep are expected" (1966, 69). Others suggest that a community is based upon relationships where everyone—administrators, teachers, and students—work together to create conditions for learning.

The concept of school as community of learners is not new. John Dewey (1916) proposed that surroundings encourage growth and talked in great detail about the impact of the learning environment upon students. He suggested that a community encourages growth by nurturing and supporting learners and by providing situations that lead to success. Dewey told us that everything that occurs in the school environment affects learning, and learning occurs when all are participants in activities. He argued that beliefs and understandings are not delivered but are communicated. This idea of communication leads to dialogue and participation in the school community. Through talking with students, we can learn about their interests, their likes and dislikes, their frustrations, and their perceptions about what works and does not work in their learning activities. I will explore the idea of dialogue in more detail in Chapter 7.

Knowledge

A key issue that educators explore in a community of learners is "What is knowledge?" According to the constructivist approach to learning, knowledge is created not discovered. Deconstructionism, as represented by Jacques Derrida, challenges the history of an event or thought. His work attempts to untangle the effect of power and language on meaning (Slattery 1995). Postmodern thought challenges the ways that knowledge is produced through the information explosion and the representation of "reality" as put forth in media and technology. There is an emphasis on autobiography and questioning text from political, gender, and racial perspectives. Curricular implications of these include changing the way teachers look at students and learning.

Mary Belenky and others identified five perspectives on knowing which they have proposed are "Women's Way of Knowing." These categorize the assumptions about truth, knowledge and authority that women demonstrate. The silent, received, subjective, and procedural categories assume a body of knowledge to be received or acted upon. However, the constructed knowledge category assumes that the knower is an intimate part of the known ((Belenky et al. 1986). The *constructed knowledge* women put an emphasis on a continual search for truth and that knowledge is relative to the person. Knowing is not a procedure but a way of life.

The influences of culture and social class on knowledge are often discussed in conjunction with feminist theory. There are several views about the ways that multiculturism affects knowledge production and curriculum and the implications of power and economics. These views, along with the feminist perspective, are entwined in the postmodern approach to knowledge (Pinar et al. 1995). Critical theory is a term used to denote alternative views including feminism and postmodernism. Critical theory can be an added dimension of constructivism. However, the "critical" in critical theory comes from the aim of inquiry that is to promote social change by the understanding of social, economic, ethnic, and gender structures.

All of these perspectives of knowledge made me wonder about the knowledge students bring to school and what knowledge is valued in the school systems. What experiences color their perceptions and how have we historically determined the "truth" of our knowledge? The book, *Lies My Teacher Told Me,* by James W. Loewen (1996) immediately came into my mind. The author challenges aspects of our culture that we have taken as "true" and gives facts that support a different truth.

Creating a Vision

I became troubled when I found that some authors believe that schools are resistant to change, and this failure to change is because educators are unwilling to address future societal needs (Betts 1992; Sarason 1990). Since our society is changing, and becoming more diverse, middle school educators are being challenged to change, to be flexible. Are we ready for the challenge?

In his book, *Changing Schools from Within,* Roland Barth (1990) suggests that school communities must establish a vision: What do we want this school to be? Schools reflect societal influences; thus they cannot change in isolation. Yet, schools cannot just respond to the needs of today; they must change to meet future needs. Schools and the social institutions within which they exist must look to the future, and it is our students who are our future.

How are each of the challenges and a school's vision affected by issues of diversity? How can we work with students in developmentally responsive ways to create school communities that meet the needs of students in a rapidly changing society? The constraints upon middle level education may appear daunting. However, those who believe in developmentally responsive middle level schools will meet the needs of the students. Academic achievement is possible, and may actually be enhanced, by a developmentally appropriate environment that builds upon diversity in a supportive learning community. Learning communities that wish to support learning and diversity together create a vision of what their school will be. In the following chapters, issues related to each challenge are discussed in depth. I will discuss the concept of community in detail in Chapter 6.

CHAPTER 3

Identity

I have fond memories of cuddling under a quilt while my grandmother told me stories. Some of the stories revolved around the fabric scraps she included in her quilts. Many brightly colored patches were scraps from dresses she or my mother wore. Others were from clothes Grandma had sewn for me. My grandmother was a widow when she raised six children in the 1930s and she wasted nothing. Her patchwork was found all around our house. I still have the quilt she made for my doll carriage and quilts she made for our beds.

Quilting is a popular hobby and, as an adult, I enjoy making my own memories. I am fascinated by putting the quilts together, choosing the fabrics, arranging and rearranging the design, and piecing the small fabric shapes to make a larger creation. I prefer to hand sew my quilts rather than use a sewing machine although a machine would be much faster. There is something about the handwork that makes the time I spend quilting much more enjoyable.

In a quilt, specific combinations of shapes are given names: the Ohio Star, Bear's Paw, and Log Cabin to name a few. An interesting fact I learned while researching quilts is that the same pattern may have different names depending upon the section of the country in which the creator lived. I am always amazed how two people can start out with the same pattern, and sometimes the same fabric, yet come out with strikingly different works of art. Quilts tell stories of families, towns, and even countries. Quilts show the influences of history on people. In a way, some of the charm of quilting seems to be disappearing. As I talk to hobby quilters, read magazines, and go to quilt shows, I find a great deal of time spent on making sure quilts are done "right." I even joke about the "quilt police" with friends as we are sure the "quilters" will reject our creations. Now many hobby quilters insist on the right fabric (100% cotton), the right thread (no polyester), and the right batting (perfect weight, shrink resistant). Gone is the charm of patches made of seed bags or worn clothing and linings from what ever was available (even worn quilts).

Identity Formation

To me, a quilt is like a person's identity. Small, sometimes seemingly incongruous pieces are slowly combined, building a beautiful creation. The individual care and love that goes into the quilt is what makes it special. Society's emphasis on the perfect body presented with impeccable taste with impeccable credentials seems like the quilt police search for a perfect quilt pattern with the perfect colors, stitches, and fabric. A person's self-image is compared against society's standard and unless the standard is met, the person is not worthy of the prize.

David Elkind (1984) referred to patchwork in a different light than I do. He referred to adolescents who had a "patchwork self" as those who have unconnected values, attitudes and habits that influence their approaches to stressful situations. He suggests that those with a patchwork self, "mismanage stress" because of their "inner conflicts" (169). Thus, Elkind and I make meaning of experience in different ways. Yes, the way the pieces of our selves are put together does influence the way we deal with situations. I see the role each attitude, habit, or value can have in the students' lives. Rather than use the term "mismanage," I like to use the term "approach." Our values, attitudes, and habits are somehow interconnected, but perhaps in a pattern that is elusive and strange. The final product may not meet the standards of the "quilt police," but it is the adolescent's pattern, the whole identity.

When I think of my own identity, I think of myself as a mother, a wife, a professor, a sister, and now a grandmother. These pieces of myself fit together to make me. I can rearrange these pieces to make different patterns, different quilts, for different parts of my life. How I define these roles, how I achieved these roles, and how I interpret the importance of these roles is based upon my experiences and assumptions. My values and attitudes have helped me address each situation I encountered. In some people's eyes, I may have mismanaged situations, yet each obstacle I encountered made me who I am today.

When I was doing my residency in my doctoral program, I had to live away from home for a year while my husband stayed in our house. One day at work someone came up to him and asked why he "allowed" me to go away for a year. My husband replied that he doesn't "allow" me to do anything; I can make up my own mind. In that person's eyes, a wife and mother shouldn't be allowed to go away. His perceptions of the role of wife and mother were different from the perceptions of my husband and myself. In my husband's co-worker's eyes, my husband and I have a strange relationship and our attitudes and values do not fit into the pattern of life expected by others. We look upon the attitudes of others as an indication of our strength and independence even though "strange."

I see adolescent identity as who the student believes himself or herself to be and where this self fits within the world. How this self is defined as an individual; as a learner; as a member of family, school or community; or as a friend depends on the interpretations the student makes of experiences and relationships with others. Identity, or self-concept, has been defined in literature as the way one sees oneself and how one interprets the way others look upon the self. According to Erikson, identity achievement is a primary goal for adolescents (1963/1998). A positive identity can encourage a student to achieve just as a negative identity may prevent the student from facing challenges (Berger 1991). Unfortunately for many students a "deterioration of self-concept as a learner occurs between third and eighth grade?" (NASSP 1989, 6) Identity development of the young adolescent is not only at a crucial stage in terms of the view of self as a learner; young adolescents worry about how they look, how they sound, and how they act.

The classroom environment becomes prominent as students develop peer relationships and seek to grow independent from adults. Usually, the young adolescent does not desire complete independence but wants to explore personal skills and values (Braddock and McPartland 1993). A classroom can provide an environment that supports their exploration through academic curriculum and exploratory activities.

Helping students develop a personal identity requires schools to provide a supportive and flexible learning environment and curriculum. Suggestions found in literature include the use of advisory groups that allow students to address developmental issues in non-threatening environments (Carnegie Council 1989; NASSP 1993; NMSA 1995). Thematic units based on questions posed by students may be structured to encourage students to explore their cultural heritages. Teachers who are knowledgeable about their students and youth culture can creatively adapt curriculum. Beyond using the techniques of effective teaching, supportive teachers develop relationships that allow students to explore their interests, beliefs, and values and thus develop understandings about who they are and how they see themselves in the world around them (Strodl 1997). How then do student identities develop in a developmentally and culturally diverse middle school environment?

Middle School Perspectives

It has often been noted that an adolescent's identity is influenced by physical development (Maynard 1986). For instance, Walker and Lirgg (1995) remind educators that middle school students typically experience a growth spurt during early adolescence that is usually associated with the onset of puberty. The most noticeable changes are in height and weight, but the body may become disproportionate. Sometimes it seems that adolescents are all feet or extremely clumsy. I often chuckle when I look at an eighth grade class and the shapes and sizes of the students. One can see a 6 foot, 175 pound boy sitting next to his 5 foot, 98 pound friend. Differences between boys and girls become accentuated. It has long been noted that girls seem to mature earlier than boys. At the fifth and sixth grade levels, especially, girls may be taller than boys. Inherent in this diversity are the problems faced by those students who are "early maturers" or "late maturers."

Early maturing boys and girls are often expected to act in manners associated with those who are older. Sometimes, the boys who are larger excel at sports and become "stars" and later, when their peers catch up, their stardom fades. Early maturing boys often are put in leadership roles that they may not be emotionally or cognitively ready to take. Early maturing girls may be the brunt of sexually suggestive jokes, get the attention of older boys, and suffer from the jealousy of their peers. In such cases, emotional and cognitive development may be out of sync with physical development.

Late maturing adolescents also have to deal with issues that may cause them angst. Boys, who are smaller than their peers, may be cut from sports teams or feel self-conscious because they are shorter than the girls. They may become the class clowns to bolster their identity or may be intimidated by those who are larger and stronger. Late maturing girls may feel inadequate and revert to acting childish or "cute." Teachers and other adults may treat these adolescents as young children and may not recognize that their intellectual and emotional development does not match their physical development.

Young adolescents must deal with adjusting their body images and accepting what their bodies look like. This concern about body image can become psychologically and physically unhealthy. Students with an obsession about the ideal body may go to extremes such as excessive dieting or taking steroids (Berger 1991). I was one of those "early maturers" who was already 5'6" in sixth grade while my classmates were much smaller. As an adolescent, I looked upon myself as "fat." Now, when I look at pictures, I really wasn't as fat as I thought!

Maynard (1986) also notes that during adolescence, psycho-social development becomes an issue when students struggle in the transition between their view of self as the center of their world and as part of their ever-expanding social context. As they move to seeing themselves as part of the world, they may also be fixated on the self (Bowers 1995). Part of this egocentrism is the imaginary audience that the young person may create. An adolescent may feel that everyone is looking at him or her. A slight blemish or the gym locker room may cause anxiety. Another egocentric dimension is often labeled the "invincibility fable"; young adolescents may take risks, thinking that they will not be hurt in dangerous situations. For this reason, young people may not heed the warnings about the dangers of drugs or tobacco (Berger 1991).

Criticism, whether real or imaginary, is an issue in psycho-social development of young adolescents as such can evoke key emotions and feelings. According to the NMSA (1995), young people tend to be self-conscious and sensitive to personal criticism. They have a growing need for peer approval as the need for adult approval decreases. However, adolescents often react strongly to embarrassment or ridicule. Even criticism by adults about their hair or their clothes can have an effect upon the students' perceptions of how teachers see and care about them.

Relationships between boys and girls and with peers can also affect identity. Differences in social development may cause anxieties when students must work together on projects or speak in front of groups. Family and home situations also affect social development, and home situations may be contrary to the norm, thus these adolescents may feel different or "weird." To deal with their own struggle with identity and to establish their relationships within the classroom, students may take on roles within the classroom: the clown, the bully, the teacher's pet, or the shy one. I will discuss the importance of relationships in more detail in Chapter 5.

The third difference among adolescents concerns emotional development, which may be affected by physical development (Maynard 1986). Often, emotional development does not correlate with physical development and students are faced with choices or experiences because of physical maturity that they are not emotionally ready to handle (Brough 1990). Other emotional pressures result from the desire for independence from parental authority. A range of feelings from inferiority to superiority contributes to the emotional diversity found among young adolescents (Maynard 1986). However, as Berger (1991) reminds us, although some studies show that during adolescence the incidence of problems such as law breaking and depression do increase over the rate that occurs in childhood, the percentage of students with serious emotional or behavioral problems is less than many people believe.

Finally, Maynard (1986) points out that great diversity is found in the intellectual development of young adolescents. Students may not develop abstract thinking as early as thought, therefore, opportunities for students to make the transition from concrete to abstract thinking must be incorporated regularly in middle school practice (Berger 1991; Slavin 1994). Students demonstrate cognitive levels that range from the pre-operational, through the concrete to the formal, more mature level. The NASSP reminds educators that intellectual development is mediated by development in other areas, and a holistic view of the learner must be recognized (1989).

As a former middle school math teacher, I am acutely aware of the differences in intellectual development during young adolescence. Mathematics is one area in which the differences regularly appear. There is a push to teach algebra in earlier and earlier grades. Not too long ago, only the gifted or "academically advanced" students studied algebra in eighth grade. Now, algebra is part of a typical eighth grade curriculum. Yet cognitively, many students are not ready for the abstract algebraic concepts. Algebra cannot be taught to these students in the same manner as it would be taught in high school. However this often happens and students are not successful. Algebraic concepts can be taught to those who are still moving from the concrete to the abstract level of thinking, but they must be taught in a more concrete manner. Adolescents want to see real-world connections and can be successful when mathematics is presented in problem-solving situations.

The four dimensions of adolescent identity identified by Maynard and supported by other middle school literature do not recognize diversity in racial, religious, or socio-economic issues nor have such issues appeared consistently in mainstream literature. Likewise, gender is not addressed in a manner that fully explores implications of societal power hierarchies that may disenfranchise some students. In schools, most studies of adolescent development, and their identity development, have stemmed from our American tradition and expectations. Cultural expectations and roles that young adolescents take within diverse cultures may make "different" students appear "developmentally delayed" or "early matured."

Erik Erikson is often considered to be the guru of understanding adolescents. According to Erikson (1963/1998), identity achievement is a primary goal for adolescents. As a developing educator, I was immersed in developmental theories and embraced the concept that my middle school students developed at different rates and that they were not all ready for the abstract "high school" approach. Although I somehow sensed other "differences," I was not critically aware of their impact. Even later in my dissertation research about student perceptions of their middle school environment, socio-economic and gender issues immerged, although cultural issues did not. But what should I have expected? All my subjects were white students from a rural area.

Gender Influences

Gender differences in identity have gained respectability due to such writers as Carol Gilligan and Margaret Pipher. *Reviving Ophelia* (Pipher 1994) hit the trade book shelves and the author did the talk show rounds and appeared on *Oprah*. William Pollack's books on boys' development, *Real Boys* (1998) and *Real Boys' Voices* (2000) have received similar attention and he, too, achieved the status of Oprah's guest. Gender differences also receive substantial mention in textbooks for educational psychology and teaching methods. Research clearly shows that girls and boys are treated differently in the classroom. Expectations for achievement and behavior are different. Teacher and student interactions are different. The sad part is that most teachers don't realize that they are treating boys and girls differently. Part of a student's identity is based upon how the student perceives that others see him or her. The subtle messages related to gender influence students' sense of worth. Sadker and Sadker's book, *Failing at Fairness: How America's Schools Cheat Girls* (1994), is a valuable resource for those who wish to explore classroom gender issues.

Gender identity is usually approached from the male-female perspective. Many textbooks only hint at the issue of gay and lesbian teenagers and the identity issues they must face. I recently reviewed a work about abnormal psychology in which such gender identities were approached as a problem, as deviant. Such perceptions about gay and lesbian students still prevail.

I have an aunt who is now in her mid-eighties and taught school for almost 40 years. One day we sat on her porch swing and in talking about this book we discussed the needs of gay and lesbian students. She believes that a teacher has the responsibility to work with any child who walks into her classroom. She told of several special students she remembered and remarked that their orientation wasn't their fault, but it was too bad that something medical couldn't be done to "fix" them. Bless her heart. When my brothers and I were in college during the 1960s and early 1970s, holey jeans were part of our uniform. I'll never forget the time when my grandmother came to visit and while my brother was out, sat and patched all his jeans. She felt she had to hide the holes, to fix the jeans so her grandson was respectable! So it is with the gender identity of many young people. They feel they must hide to be respectable and others feel they should be fixed.

Uribe and Harbeck (1992) state that a unique problem facing homosexual youth in identity development is lack of support. Because of the negative stigma of homosexuality, these students are often separated from other social aspects of their identity development in ways that others who are different are not. Young adolescence is extremely important, for at this age gender identity is not completely formed so adolescents tend to conceal their insecurities. They may tend to overcompensate for their insecurities by trying to excel at academics, dropping out of activities, or even lying about dating.

Clearly discussions of gender identity are sanitized and politically correct in educational literature. Nevertheless, cultural, linguistic, and socio-economic differences receive minor attention in middle school literature compared to the discussion of gender. Yes, roughly half of our students are boys and the other half are girls. Furthermore, according to census statistics, in the near future over 50% of our students will be non-white and nearly as many will be from homes where English is not the only language spoken. Gender roles often are culturally defined with expectations mitigated by tradition, religion, and economics. For instance, recent research suggests that the definition of masculine roles and identity is related to an African American or Latino individual's view of personal self-worth and ethnicity while European American males do not make associations with these factors because of what some have considered the impact of their "whiteness" (Abreu et al. 2000).

As teachers, we are more familiar with the roles defined by our own cultures, particularly European American, and often it is difficult to understand gender roles associated with those who are different. Do the cultures of our female students expect girls to be wives and mothers rather than corporate executives? Who are we to say that the cultural definitions of roles that are different from our definitions are wrong? As a teenager I often balked at the roles expected of me. Nevertheless, I fulfilled those roles—caretaker, decision-maker, and "young lady." Developmentally responsive middle level schools provide opportunities for exploration of culturally defined roles in a non-judgmental, supportive atmosphere.

Ethnic and Racial Influences

A year or so ago, while channel flipping on a Sunday afternoon, I came across a book-talk show featuring Elva Traviño Hart. She was presenting her book, *Barefoot Heart: Stories of a Migrant Child* (1999). She captured my imagination as she shared her childhood as a Latina migrant worker. She read portions of her book in Spanish and then read the translation. I was overcome with the beauty of her native language and the emotion I felt hearing her speak even though I remember little of my high school Spanish. I hardly listened to the English translations. The next day, I ordered the book from a local bookstore and anxiously awaited its arrival.

As an adult, Elva was troubled by her cultural identity that she cleverly hid in the corporate world where she excelled. How many others have agonized about their cultural or ethnic identity? How does this identity mold students' perceptions of themselves and impact upon their school experiences and how do school experiences mold a student's identity? What exactly is *ethnic identity*?

Ethnic identity has been defined as an individual's sense of belonging to a particular ethnic group and how the person demonstrates this group membership through actions, thoughts, and perceptions (Phinney and Cobb 1996). This identity develops through socialization within familial and community experiences. Young children first become aware of subtle differences among people such as skin color and social differences. However, it is believed that most growth in identity occurs during adolescence (Spencer et al. 2000).

Phinney (1989) proposed that adolescents' ethnic identity develops in a manner similar to Marcia's four-part developmental model: diffused, foreclosed, moratorium, and achieved identity. According to Phinney, adolescents in the diffused and foreclosed stages have not explored their ethnicity, have had few experiences in which they have encountered ethnic issues, and may have embraced their parents' attitudes and beliefs about their ethnic or cultural group without self-exploration. Students who are exploring their ethnicity but have not identified entirely with their ethnic group are considered to be in a stage of moratorium. Finally, according to Phinney, students who have achieved identity have spent time investigating their ethnicity, understand the implications of their identity, and embrace and have pride in their ethnicity.

When students enter their school years, they have a wealth of knowledge from their homes and families. We hear constantly about the national goal that every child entering school will be ready to learn. But the inference is that unless students enter with the background experiences that we expect, their background is lacking. Even I have lamented about children who enter school without knowing nursery rhymes. I never thought to ask if they knew any other stories. This is particularly important when working with diverse students. Is a Native American student deprived if he knows his family's legends rather than the story of Humpty Dumpty?

Undoubtedly, children arrive at school with different backgrounds and some with more socially acceptable knowledge than others. Nevertheless, from the beginning students learn whether their background is "good enough" and if their culture's contribution is not valued, they connect this to their personal identities. In a period when young adolescent students are eager to explore, their opportunities to explore are limited. At a time when students are anxious to address social issues and be involved in community action, their ability to develop pride in their culture is thwarted by curricula designed to support the dominant culture. In our predominately white, Christian culture, students from other cultures must negotiate differences with their own unique frames of reference.

Compounding the challenge for teachers, who may be ethnically different from their students, are differences within ethnic groups. Not all youth from the same group have the same cultural background. For example, not all Native Americans have the same perspectives. Mary Crow Dog, in her book *Lakota Woman* (1990), tells of her adolescence and her discovery of Native American traditions. Her mother embraced Catholicism and did not encourage Mary Crow Dog's interest in her Native American roots.

Those from backgrounds other than white also walk carefully between two worlds; they may feel that they dishonor their backgrounds by "acting white" or be accused of being too white by others in their peer group. The way the students negotiates this dilemma and deal with the social implications and relationships within their peer groups may have profound repercussions upon school success and relationships. These issues are discussed in greater depth in Chapters 4 and 5.

Native American identity issues are often related to their perceptions of the history of oppression in society. Adolescents must confront the ways racism and oppression impact upon their roles in society; they must reconcile how they see themselves and how they perceive others see them. Some suggest that these issues actually delay the achievement of the adolescent task of identity formation. According to some, urban Native American youth have an even more difficult time understanding their ethnic identity because they are separated from cultural resources (Cleary and Peacock 1998).

Native Americans are considered minorities but are unique because they are not immigrants. John Ogbu (1992) suggests that immigrants' perceptions are influenced by the precipitating cause of their move. Those who chose to immigrate to the United States may have different outlooks from those whose ancestors came as slaves or those who came to the United States out of desperation and were refugees from their homeland.

Studies particularly related to the issue of black student identities were not readily available until the 1970s, and those were usually considered to be deficit models suggesting minority students' cultures were substandard and the students had to be remediated. Burt and Halpin (1998) additionally point out that developmental models such as those based upon the work of Erikson were dated. Within the last half of the twentieth century, a change in the African-American identity transformed. Instead of identifying with the dominant culture and looking at themselves as lesser, black students are becoming comfortable with their own culture within the dominant culture. Recent theories of black student identity development include the work by James Banks who emphasizes the importance of acceptance of positive aspects of one's own ethnic identity.

Now, more than ever before, biracial or multiracial students are present in our classrooms, and these children often have special issues with their ethnicity and culture. Until the 1960s, biracial marriages were illegal in some states. Not until the Supreme Court Decision, *Loving v. Virginia*, did such marriages become "legitimized" in a legal sense. Nevertheless, laws do not control the emotions and attitudes of people. When children have mixed heritages, they must deal with a society that does not recognize them as individuals. Through their lives they are often asked to identify themselves with such terms as White, Black,

Native American, or other. Even our government census forms cause anxiety. How do these children fit into a classification? Should they always consider themselves as "others?" Often the students are in "no man's land" and are accepted by neither their fathers' nor mothers' communities. This is particularly evident in students whose parents are Black and White. The Asian and White parentage is more accepted than White and Black (Burns 1998). Although some research has been completed about the identity development of biracial, multiracial, and multiethnic adolescents, and has found there are particular issues related to this identity development, there clearly is much more work to be done (Spencer et al. 2000).

Socio-economic Influences

Identity development is dynamic and multidimensional; no one piece of a person's self-concept works in isolation. Brantlinger (1993) and others propose that economic status is a dimension within which differences such as gender and ethnicity are compounded. According to Brantlinger, social class is integral in adolescent identity development. Social class influences the students' perceptions of school situations and achievement and has definite effects on peer relationships. Low-income students in Brantlinger's study expressed feelings of futility and lack of power within the system. These same students believed that teachers had a lower opinion of them than of high-income students. Both high-income and low-income students expressed the opinion that teachers treated students differently based on their economic or social background. Some research suggests that student perceptions are close to reality. Davis (2001) found that teachers' perceptions of students' academic abilities are related to the students' social and interpersonal abilities.

School practices such as tracking appeared to have an impact upon students' perceptions of themselves. Students in Brantlinger's study voiced the opinion that being put in a lower track labeled them as inferior in ability. Furthermore, Brantlinger's students remarked that teachers' attempts to hide the level of groups by giving groups clever names did not work as the names often became sources of ridicule. Often students from lower income situations masked their feelings of vulnerability by assuming a self-image of toughness (1993). Their bravado belies the insecurities and confusion that they often face with their peers and adults. Similar perceptions about social class and tracking were found in Eder's study (1994).

What Do Students Have to Say?

Much of what the students said in the study I conducted in 1998 was consistent with what Brantlinger, Eder, and others said. The students in my study did not bring in ethnic or racial issues, but they were not faced with these issues themselves. The students were concerned about how the teachers perceived them. One student told me, "This goes for sports in school but if like your parents own a business or are rich or something most of the time you'll be one of their star players. Not all the time, but you know what I mean. And then like at school, they're the teacher's main choice. The teachers always pick them."

Students were concerned about what teachers thought of them. One student told me, "I was told before that they will like tell other teachers cause they have meetings all the time and they will like tell each other and they're going to have this kid next year…[teacher] even said that she told her husband, 'Oh, you are going to have this kid. He writes really sloppy…and tell him if he writes sloppy next year you'll give him a zero.' … Your reputation will follow you, because of last year. They might not like someone because they were kinda bad. I have another reason. They were sitting there saying they knew my sister. They say, I knew your sister." This student was clearly concerned about what teachers thought of him.

Another issue that students brought up was criticism. Students were sensitive and vulnerable to the criticism of adults, a typical young adolescent response. This conversation was in the midst of a discussion.

> [I would like] freedom not to be judged…Like if I want to wear my hair …like weird…like I don't know…like my hair one day…All the teachers hated it…They told me they hated it.
> It was cute. I liked it.

> Like we would be happier if we could...
> If we weren't criticized
> Yeah, criticized.

Even though gender issues were not a focus in my 1998 study, eighth graders interjected the topic of "sexist" into our conversations. In one session, both girls and boys described their perceptions of teachers who appeared to show gender bias.

Very judgmental...Like if you don't like football...they're sexist too.
Yeah, sexist; very sexist.
What do you mean sexist?
Favors guys over girls...for guys
Favors guys
Not me. I told him I don't like football.
He favors guys over girls because they can do football.
Yeah, there's certain guys he doesn't like.
He's friendly to them but he just likes them more.

We're not like he wants us to be...We don't like football ...and I don't know...I don't know...we just don't like the things he does.

I wanted to play football in 6th and he [the teacher] told the boys I shouldn't be able to play...I was in football when I was in 6th grade like when he first saw me he didn't think I should be playing. He didn't like me because I was a girl and all but now...but now...
He bugs her all the time.

I think all the good teachers are guys...actually I have one favorite that is a girl...but they're always better to all the girls...I have a girl teacher and she's prejudice and she only likes girls and hates guys and that's why I don't like her... Some of the teachers, like I said before, they like girls better than guys...and it is the other way around too. The guys like boys better cause they are guys and stuff like that. Like [teacher] will be really kind to the girls and be "nananana get over here" to boys. We'll be doing the same things that they are doing, but she will yell at us and leave them alone.

Did you notice that all the main parts [in a project] went to guys? A lot of it was just guys but instead of having...oh wow... all the main parts were guys...and if you didn't get a part...It was mostly girls...mainly...Most of the people got a part but most of the people that didn't were girls...but all the guys got parts.

Students in my study used football as a frame of reference. Football, a typically male sport, was the determining factor of whether some students were "liked" by teachers in the students' eyes. These students described situations that are strikingly similar to what Myra and David Sadker reported in their study, *Failing at Fairness: How America's School Cheat Girls* (1994). This study, and many others, found that teachers may not be acutely aware of their behaviors, but they do tend to treat boys and girls differently in the classroom.

Challenge

Identity then is how one puts together the pieces of oneself (gender, racial, ethnic, and socio-economic) in a unique pattern to present oneself to the world. According to the NMSA (1995), students wish to be valued members of the school community and they want to be valued as individuals. Young adolescents struggle daily to develop their own identity. We must return to the theories of adolescent development that remind us that middle school students seeking to become independent still look to adults for guidance and as models of behaviors and attitudes. It is up to the teacher to acknowledge the individuality of the students within the classroom.

In her seminal book, *The Challenge to Care in Schools* (1992), Nel Noddings challenges educators to find opportunities to help students learn to care for themselves, to appreciate their own talents and limitations, to learn about the emotional, spiritual and intellectual facets of their own personal identities, and to explore their potentials. The teachers that Gloria Ladson-Billings describes in her book, *The Dreamkeepers: Successful Teachers of African American Children* (1994), do just that. Ladson-Billings suggests that culturally relevant teaching can help students achieve while developing a positive African American identity. These teachers, who may or not be Black, empower students to be successful within the dominant culture while recognizing their culture as a legitimate part of the curriculum. How do teachers in developmentally and culturally diverse middle schools come to terms with students' individual identities in order to provide a learning environment that supports students?

Reflection upon one's own professional practice enables those who wish to provide support for all of their students in the learning environment. The foregoing examples of diversity that may be found among the students in a middle level school indeed presents a challenge to educators who interact with students on a daily basis. It is the adults within the school environment who have been challenged to address students' needs in a developmentally responsive way, certainly not an easy task. However, an appreciation of student diversity forms a foundation for the building of a learning community that provides experiences that promote the development of students' individual identities as learners, as members of families, school, and community, and as friends. In the next chapter, the intersection of identity and success will be discussed.

CHAPTER 4

Success

When I was little, I liked to get stars on my papers. In first grade I cried if I didn't have stars to take home. Grades were important to me. In fifth and sixth grade I had a special friend, a walk-to-school-together-Girl-Scout-camp friend. She and I competed for the top grades in our class. Sometimes I would have the top grades and sometimes she would, but we were still friends. We went to junior high school together; there were more competitors and I still liked to come on top. I was sensitive, too. When I was in ninth grade, I can remember crying at home because some other students told me that the honors I won were not the result of me being a good student but because my aunt was a teacher in the school.

I left that school after junior high and went to a much larger senior high school. I became one of many and lost in the crowd. This time the competitors weren't other students; the competitors were the teachers and the system. In tenth grade my history teacher announced that no one ever got 100% on his tests and he was proud of it. On my first test I got a D. This set the stage for a challenge. I was stubborn, and no one *told me I couldn't* get the top score. I was going to prove him wrong. I figured out his system and on the next test, I almost won. I had a 99%. He marked one answer wrong because I forgot to cross a "t"—a spelling mistake in his eyes. In my eyes, it was just a way for him to win. The next time, I won. I got the 100.

Teachers and the system—I learned how to play their games. At a class reunion several years ago, friends reminded me about how I used to give them answers to questions on tests. Not many of my close friends were in classes with me, but in chemistry one of my friends was there. She was struggling but the class came easy for me. I remember one time in particular when she was called to the board to balance some equations; she just could not understand and by the time she returned to her seat, she was in tears. I was upset and angry. I watched her take the next test and when I saw that she was in trouble, I carved the solution to the equation on the side of a pencil and conveniently dropped it so she could pick it up. I didn't care whether this was dishonest or not. The most important thing to me was my friend. I wasn't competing against her; I was helping her.

As I have learned more about myself and about adolescent development, I think about Carol Gilligan's perspectives on moral development and my adolescent ethical decisions. Were they made based upon relationships and caring rather than ideas about "cheating?" I don't remember thinking about right and wrong. My reflections may have prompted readers to reflect upon their own adolescent experiences with success. As we look at our own assumptions, we can think about how middle school philosophy is related to issues of student success and what factors may influence success.

Middle School Perspectives

According to the Carnegie Council (1989), middle level schools should provide opportunities for success for all students. The other major organizations have similar positions. Students should have the opportunity to be successful or be experts at something. The National Middle School Association states that students are capable of more success than adults assume (1995).

Developmentally appropriate middle schools have defining characteristics. An effective middle school avoids the "star system" where few students capture all the attention (George and Shewey 1994). Individual progress is emphasized more than comparisons with other students (NMSA 1995). Moos (1991) also proposed that a supportive learning environment provides opportunity for personal development and a positive environment is related to academic achievement. Student perceptions of their learning environment have been shown to have a direct relationship to learning outcomes (Fraser 1990; 1994). According to constructivist theory and middle school philosophy, in a supportive environment that promotes student success, teachers engage in learning with their students and provide help to students; materials and time are differentiated, and the curriculum is relevant to students' lives (Fraser 1990; NMSA 1995).

Having high expectations for all students is also part of middle school philosophy according to the National Middle School Association (1995) and other organizations. The standards movement throughout our nation also holds this to be a goal. In the literature, we are told that students should be told what the expectations are and to what level we expect them to achieve. In many schools and states, students are required to pass tests in order to graduate from high school or to move from one grade to another. In developmentally responsive middle level schools, educators struggle to reconcile such standards and expectations with their knowledge of adolescent development.

Middle school students have a wide range of intellectual development and some may be at a concrete level of thinking while others are transitioning into more abstract levels of thinking. They may be disinterested in traditional academic subjects. The transition from small elementary schools to larger middle schools may also be intimidating to young adolescent, and thus their success may be affected (NMSA 1995).

Earlier, I proposed that the task of middle level schools is to provide opportunities to define, work toward, and experience success in developmentally appropriate skills and knowledge. This prompts us to ask: How do gender, race and ethnicity, language, socio-economic, and learning environment factors influence student success? Who defines success? How is that success defined? How do we measure success?

Grades and Rewards

Grades were my salvation. I felt inadequate or inferior in most of my high school life. In my academic section, many of my classmates had parents who were college professors or businesspersons in town. I felt that I didn't belong. Socially and economically I was different. I took consolation in getting good grades. What I was learning didn't really matter. In fact, in most of my classes I wasn't even interested in what I was learning. I just wanted to get the grade.

My younger brothers seemed to have a different attitude. School and grades were not important. A teacher announced in front of one brother's class during his senior year that our parents were wasting their money sending him to a university; he'd never make it through his freshman year. The school called my parents and told them he couldn't graduate if he didn't start coming to school. (He now holds a Ph.D. in education and is a school administrator.) My other brother regularly skipped school to attend Pittsburgh Pirates home games and got Cs in school while at home he explained my college anthropology assignments to me. (He is a retired military officer and a state-level attorney). They didn't play the system, but they seem to be successful in their adult lives.

The teachers and the system—I learned to play their games: please the teacher and get good grades. I was successful when I competed against the teachers and the system in high school, but I almost lost the battle in college. My will to compete was gone; I felt inadequate and out of place. I remember my anthropology course. I didn't even know what anthropology was before I was enrolled in the class. The last row of seats in the class was filled with fraternity guys. I was shocked to learn that they had copies of tests to study.

English composition class was particularly frustrating. I would work hours on a paper and get it back with no "red marks" but with cryptic messages like "I don't agree with you—D." My mother told me to talk to the professor and ask for help. I got a quick brush off and never went back. Geography wasn't much better. Class was held in the music auditorium and there were 180+ students in the class. We sat alphabetically and with my last name, I ended up in the back. The professor rambled on while he used overheads that were impossible to read from the back. I frantically took notes and had no idea what he was talking about. After a visit to his office for help, I still was lost. He talked in a vocabulary that made no sense to me. I could not seem to pass the tests. I remember trying to memorize all the countries in the world and their locations for a map part of the final. I ended up with a D in the course.

The education methods classes seemed to be an endless parade of lesson plans and bulletin boards. What we were doing seemed so insignificant. I had to worry about how I was going to pay for my books the next term. There were people I knew going to Vietnam. There were race issues in the news. I remember riding through Detroit just a few weeks after the riots of 1967. I don't even remember talking about the issues in my classes.

The competition in college was different than in high school, too. My dad was ill a good portion of the time and my mom had difficulty dealing with this emotionally. His income was cut dramatically. Mom didn't drive a car and I had two younger brothers. I remember being the one who accompanied my father to the hospital in the middle of the night and at 19 years old talking to the doctor about my dad's medical condition and needs. I felt that I was holding the family together.

Who cared about grades? What did the grades mean anyway? I just wanted to get out and get a job. So that is how I looked at grades. I graduated and began my teaching career. I moved across the state to a community where I knew no one and started teaching. I was told several years after I landed that first job that I was hired because I came from a college across the state. Most of the teachers in the district were from a nearby college and the district wanted to hire people with a "different background."

As a teacher I learned that some students didn't react well to the carrot of getting good grades or "extra credit points." It took me a long time to realize this. Through experience and investigation, I learned teachers and students may look at grades and success differently and often these differences are based upon developmental, racial, social, cultural, or gender perspectives. I learned that not everyone has a dictionary or even a newspaper at home. I learned that not every family sees education as essential for success. I learned to look at my students' view of success from their perspectives not mine.

Motivation

The need to be on top is still engrained in me. I settled into a comfortable role as family caregiver and teacher. Nevertheless, my own goals and dreams again emerged. In graduate school I tormented my family and myself as I was determined to show that I was capable. I don't know whether I was trying to show others or just trying to convince myself that I deserved the degrees. Recently, a colleague and I discussed this need to achieve. She completed a doctoral program in which there were no grades; a student either passed or failed. I don't know how I would have reacted in such a program, but I know that I thrived in an academically competitive atmosphere.

As I learned more about cooperation and competitiveness, I considered different ways of teaching and learning. In one of the undergraduate courses I now teach, we do not emphasize grades but personal goals and attainment of those goals. Students in the course have a wide range of experiences and come from many disciplines. Yet, they all need to meet the standards necessary for secondary teacher certification. Students are asked to set individual goals at the beginning of the course, develop action plans, and reflect upon their own growth. There are no tests, but students must each complete a final project that demonstrates their ability to meet certification standards. For some students the course is frustrating at first. They have never been asked to take control of their own learning; they are used to homework, lectures, and being told what to do and when to do it. Others say that the format of the course is liberating. Most of the students are successful; they remark that they are amazed at what they were able to accomplish. In fact, most of them accomplish more than I expect. We struggle through because we are in a system that requires that I report grades. This is a difficult task for me and I anguish over the grades. The students seem so excited about their work and their progress but they also realize that I must evaluate them against a standard. I often wonder what has motivated the students in the class. Are they motivated to learn for learning's sake or is it the possibility of getting an A? To what do they attribute their success or lack of success?

As I studied motivation theories I encountered discussions of attribution theories that propose that students explain their success in achievement situations to ability, effort, task difficulty, or luck. Students who succeed would like to explain their success as the result of ability or effort. Students who fail would like to explain their failures as the result of bad luck or task difficulty. These attributions are related to the students' perceptions of their locus of control. A student with an internal locus of control is likely to attribute success or failure to his or her own abilities or effort. A student with an external locus of control is likely to attribute success or failure to outside factors such as luck. This sounds like a plausible theory, but it still doesn't answer my question about what makes some students successful and others not. There must be more to "motivation" than how students "attribute" their success and failure.

We reward students who meet our expectations with grades, honor roles, and honor societies. Perhaps there has been an overemphasis on such rewards and recognition. Gordon Vars (1997) suggests that an overemphasis on extrinsic rewards may turn students into "grade junkies" which emphasizes the "pay me" attitude in society (44). Alfie Kohn agrees and presents a convincing argument in his book, *Punished by Rewards: The Trouble with Gold Stars, Incentive Plans, A's, Praise, and Other Bribes* (1993/1999). According to Kohn, the use of rewards actually results in reactions opposite to what really is anticipated. He claims that behaviorist theories have conditioned students to be extrinsic rather than intrinsic learners. Students are manipulated to work for the rewards rather than the learning teachers seek. Rewards are used to control students rather than guide students.

Kohn also argues that rewards lose their effectiveness. For instance, students receive awards so frequently beginning in the early grades that by the time they get to the middle grades, special awards for good work become meaningless. He suggests that rewards and grades that encourage competition result in disrupting relationships. Furthermore, Kohn argues, rewards discourage risk-taking; students try to figure out exactly what the teacher wants and do that rather than produce original and creative products. Recently, I learned of a small rural school that is embroiled in controversy because the high school has decided to eliminate the designations of senior class valedictorian and salutatorian to eliminate the unhealthy competition within the class. If grades and rewards are not used as motivation for some students, what does motivate students to achieve?

The difference between intrinsic and extrinsic motivation and the relationship to adolescent characteristics is addressed in middle school philosophy. According to the National Middle School Association (1995), middle school students do like to have recognition for their efforts and achievements and may react negatively to criticism. They have a strong need for approval and may be discouraged easily. They are concerned about the acceptance of their peers and tend to be self-conscious and lack self-esteem. However, in their moral development they are in a transition from self-interest to being concerned for others. They are curious and anxious to learn new things, but the sustainability of their interest is low. In general, they are moving toward a desire to make the world better and take part in real-life projects.

For many reasons, it seems that there is no magic trick for motivating middle school students. Because there is a wide range in their intellectual, social, emotional, and moral development, motivation may be confusing to educators. Adding to the confusion are other issues: gender, socio-economic, and cultural. Individual differences will have a major impact upon the approach toward success taken in middle school classrooms.

Gender Influences

I learned that academic successes of boys are often attributed to intellect while girls' academic successes may be attributed to efforts or good luck (Sadker and Sadker 1994; Walkerdine 1994). Lack of success by girls is often due to a lack of confidence; girls may feel they are not smart enough to fulfill their career dreams. During adolescence, academic success of many girls diminishes (Manning 1993; Pipher 1994). It has been suggested that girls may believe that good grades hinder their popularity (Pipher 1994; Bowers 1995); popularity may be more important to young adolescent girls than academic success (Bowers

1995; Eder 1995; Pipher 1994; Sadker and Sadker 1994). Academic success was a substitute for popularity for me.

Sadker and Sadker found that girls hesitate to volunteer answers in class, often out of fear that if they volunteer wrong answers they will appear dumb, or if they volunteer correct answers they will appear too smart and others won't like them. I didn't volunteer answers because I didn't feel that my answers were "valuable." Sadker and Sadker suggest that girls try to be inconspicuous in classrooms (1994). I just felt invisible.

When success is linked with a loss of femininity and qualities, such as clear decision making and autonomous thinking, are associated with masculinity, the qualities often are not valued by girls (Gilligan 1982). It has been suggested that teachers often underestimate the intelligence of girls and instead attribute the success of girls to hard work or else comment on the form or appearance of the work produced by girls rather than the content or quality (Sadker and Sadker 1994). Sadker and Sadker also found in their studies that teachers, when asked to name outstanding students, seemed to remember boys more often than girls. Boys tend to stand out, either as very good or very bad, while girls tend to blend in and do their work quietly.

Girls have been found to refrain from competitive activities when their success depends on the defeat of others (Gilligan 1982; Pipher 1994). Girls and women experience their own value and effectiveness when they are involved in activities that encourage their relationships with others (Herr 1996). An emphasis on competition, either in academics or sports, does not support the development of collaborative relationships necessary for a supportive learning environment.

Women's anti-competitive nature, according to Gilligan (1982), is problematic in that women see things differently. There is a conflict between femininity and success, especially when success is measured in someone else's failure. Anti-competitive values do not only hinder girls. In Native American traditions, mastery is often exhibited in achievement of personal goals not comparison with others. The culture holds that all must be competent and the success of all must be celebrated. Intrinsic rather than extrinsic rewards are valued (Cleary and Peacock 1998).

In *Real Boys: Rescuing Our Sons from the Myths of Boyhood* (1998), William Pollack suggests that some boys are crushed by competition with their peers based on society's image of masculinity and they have little energy left to succeed academically. He reminds his readers that the number of boys who are in remedial programs and the number of boys who are *not* in graduate school programs indicate that schools are not addressing the needs of boys. The macho boy image is fostered; boys who may exhibit effeminate characteristics are pressured to act in stereotypical male ways while denying their own feelings. Conversely, boys who exhibit stereotypical male mannerisms sometimes are denying their own emotions and experiencing frustration. In either case, needs of young boys may conflict with their academic success. Sadker and Sadker (1994), while challenging schools to meet the needs of girls, also report that developmental needs of boys are also neglected and many times expectations for behavior and achievement are disadvantageous to boys. Furthermore, students' self-conceptions of peer relationships have been shown to affect their success (Slavin 1994). Thus, it follows that when boys and girls perceive that others perceive them negatively, their success may be hampered.

Ethnic and Racial Influences

Too many schools have fostered an environment that honors competitiveness which promotes the idealization of the individual and the development of an unhealthy emphasis on self-interest rather than the relationships which lead to a democratic, community-oriented school (Apple and Beane 1995). Gloria Ladson-Billings (1995) explains that "culturally relevant" teachers encourage a community of learners rather than competitive, individual achievement. This type of pedagogy does not "exoticize" culturally diverse students but supports their academic achievement (483).

John Ogbu (1992) suggests that conditions that influence school achievement include historical and cultural contexts. A cultural frame of reference may lead members of a minority group to interpret the situations they meet in schools in different ways. Cultural norms embraced by students and their families may encourage educational strategies that may or may not lead to success as defined by the dominant cultural norms. The cultural framework of students may influence the value placed upon the educational goals of the school, consciously or unconsciously (Huang 1993).

Ira Shor (1992) suggests that students, because of gender or ethnicity, may be put into positions where they must choose between their cultural roots and success; they may painfully forsake their minority group's attitudes and values and adopt the dominant discourse. The ways teachers react to students' cultures can have a positive or negative effect. Disregard for students' cultural backgrounds disenfranchises students and denies opportunities for success. At times, this becomes more problematic when the teacher, who may be a member of the same cultural group, mimics mannerisms and attitudes of the dominant culture and holds low expectations of the students (Anyon 1995).

Ethnicity may be linked to language differences. There are many approaches to education for non-English speaking students. Exemplary programs use students' native languages as a foundation for learning English. According to McLaughlin and McLeod (1996), program flexibility is essential in meeting the needs of linguistically diverse students. Students and teachers use language in a variety of ways depending upon the purpose and needs of the students. With careful planning and support for students, the transition to English can be successful without diminishing the value of the students' native languages. Suggestions made by the National Center for Research on Cultural Diversity and Second Language Learning (McLaughlin and McLeod 1996) include the use of cooperative learning, teams, flexible use of time, thematic approaches to content, and higher level thinking activities. These suggestions are consistent with the tenets of middle school philosophy.

Asian Americans are often characterized as intense, academically superior students who study engineering, mathematics, or physics. Many times they have been referred to as the "model minority." Goyette and Xie (1999) identified several commonalities among Asian American ethnic groups: Their small numbers make them a marginal group; they can be distinguished easily from other minority groups; they often speak their native language at home; they maintain their ethnic identities after several generations; and they view education as important to achieve success.

Goyette and Xie suggest that, although statistics may show that Asian Americans do better on standardized tests as a group, this result may not be due to innate abilities. They propose that the differences are mitigated by the high expectations held for the students and the emphasis put on their academic success. Education as a means of success is valued highly among many Asian families as a way to overcome the hurdles faced by immigrant families (1999). Nevertheless, studies as those described here do not tell the whole story. The classification of Asian is stereotypical. We fail to consider the many countries from which Asian students came. Japan, China, Korea, Vietnam are just a few. Each group of immigrants has its own set of values, beliefs, and needs.

According to Ascher (1989), contrary to the stereotype, many Southeast Asian students do not do well in school. This is particularly true for adolescents who immigrated after the age of 11 as they do not only have the stress of relocation, but they have the stress of identity development. Ascher contends that the lack of success that some of them exhibit is not only related to a mismatch of instructional programs to the students' needs but also to a mismatch in cultural perspectives of behaviors related to schooling; the Southeast Asian students are uncomfortable with the more relaxed behavior expectation that they encounter.

Language diversity has an effect on academic success. Perceptions which ethnically marginalized students have about themselves may be a function of their language and communication skills; as students struggle to learn a second language, their perceptions of their ability suffers (Dwivedi 1996). Not only do they struggle linguistically, but their cultural heritage may also be devalued, especially in an English-only setting (Anyon 1995; Bartolomé 1997; Huang 1993; Nieto 1994). This diversity, when combined with poverty can have additional effects upon the success of students.

Socio-economic Influences

Battistich and others (1995) suggest that some disadvantaged students have high aspirations or goals but feel that these goals are unattainable. Sometimes such students may form groups that hold anti-achievement values to fulfill their needs to belong and develop a group identity. These researchers remind their readers that students who live in poverty are especially vulnerable and are more successful in a school community that is supportive and caring; negative effects of poverty are mitigated in a caring school community. Entwisle, Alexander, and Olson (1997) propose an issue that is not always mentioned when discussing the socio-economic impact on student success. They suggest that stress often accompanying low income affects the lives of students at home and in school. This stress could impact upon parenting styles and relationships and ultimately the students' success in school. In periods of economic insecurity and downsizing of industry, often the economic resources of families can change dramatically and those students who have been accustomed to economic advantages may not understand the implications of economics on their daily lives. This disruption and confusion may have a direct effect on student success.

Jonathan Kozol has been an advocate for students who are socially and economically disenfranchised and the schools they attend. Through his books, he gives insight into school communities that do not have the resources to support high standards. He describes science classes that have no labs, classrooms that have no textbooks, and schools that have poor heating and plumbing. He argues that students in these schools do not have the resources to compete with those who have advantages. The students also receive a message about their worthiness (1991).

Angela McRobbie (1991) suggests that the intersection of gender and socio-economic factors also can be connected to the difference between the goals and success of boys and girls. Working-class girls, she suggests, are less likely to have academic aspirations than girls who are from higher economic levels. She also suggests their goals are influenced by popular media such as music, film, and magazines. The racial, economic, and gender roles portrayed through these formats encourage the romantic, subservient role for women and promote the male as the wage earner.

Edwin Farrell (1990) states that adolescents' success in school is related to two factors, literacy and attitude. He suggests that the amount of exposure to literacy sources is directly related to success. He says that those students who have had to struggle, often with limited resources, have developed a negative attitude toward school. Additionally, he adds social isolation to the equation. Thus, economic situations that have a direct relationship to availability of resources and social contacts impact upon student success.

Curriculum

Through cultural images, students encounter knowledge about the way it's "supposed" to be. This knowledge of traditions, often based on ideals and visions, may be divorced from the reality of school. Curriculum frequently does not match the experiences of students in relationship to their lives outside of school. This includes the tangible, overt, curriculum of textbooks and curriculum guides as well as the subtle, hidden curriculum of the day-to-day school life (Anyon 1995; Huang 1993; Nieto 1994; Sadker and Sadker 1994; Taylor, Dawson, and Fraser 1995). Students and teachers both benefit when curriculum is built upon the cultural or experiential background which students bring to school (Bartolomé 1997; Nieto 1994). Learning increases when differences are acknowledged and examined (Robertson 1996). Historically, schools have been dominated by a Euro-American, androcentric orientation. Failing to acknowledge the need to change perpetuates the status quo (Anderson and Burns 1989). Even when the appearance of change is present, traditional ideologies persist (Arnot 1994; Pinar et al. 1995).

Schools often neglect to bring up sensitive issues about race, gender, or culture, especially when those issues conflict with the dominant culture which in effect silences those views. This in essence legitimizes racism, discrimination, or other related topics (Nieto 1994). The choices that are made as to which voices are legitimized and which voices are not is a political statement about the values and beliefs to be honored. By neglecting history and culture of some, the empowerment of all students is threatened (Shor 1992). By giving voice to all participants, the curriculum can be enriched and success, not only academic but also social, can be supported. A comparative view of cultures which explores the cultural frames of reference of all students can promote success, not only as defined by the dominant culture, but as defined by the students' cultural heritage (Gresson 1997).

In-depth discussions about the diversity that students have in racial, ethnic, religious, gender, or socio-economic status do not often appear within literature about programs for adolescents (Carnegie Council 1989; Maynard 1986; NASSP 1989, 1993; NMSA 1995) nor are educators consciously aware of the impact of differences (Gresson 1997). Schools are part of a larger social system. Not only do they reflect issues in society, they perpetuate the status quo. Those who support multicultural education for social action and change look at the power structures and situations that exist and develop curriculum that encourages change.

Marilyn Cochran-Smith (1995) cautions that it is not appropriate to believe that pedagogy can be developed that prescribe specific activities that can be applied across all schools and communities. Such practices tend to negate the idea of cultural diversity and support the development of stereotypes and alienate many of those whose diversity is purportedly acknowledged. Groups of individuals must not be essentialized. Although we must be careful not to stereotype students, cultural traits exist and knowledge of these traits may enhance a teacher's ability to support all students.

Linguistic diversity is on the rise and the importance of language in academic, social, and economic success cannot be minimized. Language is a primary element of a student's cultural capital—the knowledge of what to say, how to say it, and when it is appropriate to say. Language and culture cannot be divided (Sulentic 2001). It is through language that culture, values, and traditions are communicated. Language is also an aspect of one's personal and cultural identity.

In a *Multicultural Education* article, Margaret-Mary Sulentic (2001) chronicled her experiences as a white teacher as she encountered Black English in

Waterloo, Iowa. As a language arts teacher, she struggled to understand the cultural and historical framework of the language system used by many of her students. Her challenge, like mine with the "barn talk," was helping students negotiate between home and school language. As she emphasized, language was a vehicle of power; being able to use language of the dominant culture enabled students to cross borders within the community.

It is becoming common for school districts to serve children from as many as 60 to 100 linguistically diverse backgrounds. In many cases students may not speak English yet they are bilingual or multilingual. Students may or may not be "literate" in their own language. This compounds the issues in the classroom. Ellen and Jeffrey Kottler suggest in their book *Children with Limited English* (2002) that the terms *English as a Second Language (ESL)* and *bilingual* are becoming obsolete. They suggest that a more appropriate term would be *English Language Learners (ELL)*. *Bilingual* or even *multilingual*, according to the Kottlers, suggests that students are literate in the languages. They prefer the term "children with limited English" to describe those who are not at the point in their English language development that their native English-speaking peers who have native English-speaking parents.

Language is socially developed. The learning environment expands from the home environment to the school environment. I can remember my "baby" using a word that we never used at home and telling me that he heard it from the kids on the bus. Children construct their knowledge of language by experiencing and interacting with others. They need to make sense of the language. It is also language that opens doors to knowledge and opportunity. Educational jargon can quickly dishearten someone who wants to learn about theory and put it into practice. Furthermore, that same educational jargon can confuse and turn away parents. Many parents, especially those who have negative memories of school themselves, may not come to conferences because they feel inadequate to converse in the language of school.

Language can open or close doors to opportunities. Recently, I heard a career counselor speak about programs he had to help students learn to interact in the corporate world. He taught them how to act and talk so they wouldn't embarrass themselves and so they could get the jobs they wanted. Schools must help students negotiate the transition between cultural language with which students are comfortable and the language of the dominant culture. Language is intertwined with economics.

In developmentally and culturally responsive middle level schools, curriculum and assessments are examined and redefined; new assessment approaches that reflect real learning tasks are investigated. Support is provided for students who need more time or encouragement to learn; programs that meet developmental needs nourish strengths and overcome weaknesses of individual students (Carnegie Council 1989). Both the overt and hidden curricula reflect cultural differences. Students have a clear understanding of what standards and expectations are; they understand the target and believe they can reach it. They are able to measure their own progress toward the goals.

Assessment

High expectations and standards are essential in our challenging world. If one is to believe that students are not achieving at the level we would like, we must explore why this is so. Students may have more skills and knowledge than we believe because the curriculum does not allow them to demonstrate the skills (Beane 1993; NMSA 1995). The Carnegie Council for Adolescent Development reminds all that the cognitive development of adolescents is not "on hold" and that students have the capacity for "active engaged thinking" and a disposition toward inquiry, discovery, and reasoning across all subject areas (1989, 43). Adolescents exhibit a wide range of cognitive abilities. Because these young people are at varying stages of development, some may be thinking at a concrete level while others are able to think abstractly (Maynard 1986). This is not an indication of their potential but of their stages of development. Just as some children are slow to begin walking but may eventually win a race, some students are not ready for the tasks that we ask them to do. They need support as they learn and grow into their potentials.

As a society, we have equated academic success with scores on tests designed to measure achievement in a time- and cost-efficient manner. We overwhelm students and parents with computer printouts of stanine, percentile, and grade equivalent scores. We set levels of achievement and conduct statistical analyses based on norm groups, sampling, and levels of significant differences. As many studies suggest, a large number of students are not meeting our level of expectation. At this point, educators must look at what is assessed and how it is assessed. Do assessments meet the instructional goals and values espoused by educators or are they designed to placate the critics?

Minority groups and those from lower socio-economic levels are over-represented in under-achieving groups (George and Alexander 1993; Weissert 1999). There is a concern that a national curriculum and testing program will lead to an increasing number of at-risk students who struggle with school achievement (NASSP 1993). In many cases advantaged students are considered successful when assessed by traditional methods. However, when "at risk" students are deemed unsuccessful, schools do not consider that the failure of minority or low-income students may be the result of inappropriate curriculum, pedagogy, or assessment (Oakes, Vasudeva, and Jones 1996). Especially troubling are reports that minority students, regardless of their socio-economic status, are not achieving at their potential (Weissert 1999).

Standards communicated by adults mold the perceptions students have of their own abilities (Horn 1996). Often teachers convey low expectations unknowingly by attitudes or casual remarks (Davies 1995; NMSA 1995). We tell students we don't have high expectations when they are assigned to lower tracks from which they cannot escape. Students are traditionally assigned to tracks based upon their achievement on standardized tests and disadvantaged youth are often disproportionately found in the lower tracks (Carnegie Council 1989). We forget about the students who may have other talents and may be successful in their developmentally appropriate skills that may lead them to a healthy and productive life.

Curriculum, pedagogy, and assessment are inseparable. As we develop curriculum to address the needs of all students, we must remember that the methods to teach that curriculum must vary as must the way we assess student progress. Students may attain high standards in many different ways; unfortunately, the standards movement seems to be encouraging standard methods. Schools are requiring specific lessons be taught to all students, and teachers are afraid to vary from the prescription. In developmentally responsive middle level schools, educators consider standards in light of the needs and development of the students and high expectations are held for all.

What Do Students Have to Say?

I asked students in my study what would help them be more successful; they gave me many suggestions. One of the issues students talked about was the need for the amount of time to learn being adjusted to meet student needs. "Like we have one lesson a day and he has to rush it so he can get through it every day and then he doesn't have the time to talk over and let us really understand it...as soon as he gets that part of the notes done, he hands a paper out and usually the bell rings and he hands the paper out and we usually run out of time." Conversely, the students appreciated teachers who were sensitive to the need for some students to have more time to learn a concept. "He took the whole period to teach us." Among their suggestions were, "Slow it down." Another student added, "They need to take the time...extra time to help us like explain things better or something."

Another issue students raised was that they wanted to have teachers be willing to help with their work. One student said, "...a lot of students need more help than they get, but they don't feel like asking for it because they get embarrassed when people make fun of them for asking for help." Other remarks included: "They'll [the teachers] say we already went over it." "They make you feel stupid." "Sometimes you get in trouble for asking. They say if you ask questions.... We already went over that. That's all they say." "...there would be tons more teachers for a class so that the students would get the help that they need by themselves...cause now the teachers have to run from one person, to the next person, to the next person."

Teachers helping students is clearly a topic for which these students had strong feelings. The students in my group seemed to believe that teachers did not understand them, teachers did not have time to help them, or teachers did not want to help them. Sometimes students were hesitant to ask for help. Students were also vocal about the way they were taught. They wished for more student-teacher interaction in the classroom rather than teacher-talk. The students' perceptions support the social learning aspect of constructivist learning.

Students also told me that school would be more interesting if they had some choice about what they would be studying. "If we picked what we want, it would be more interesting." "Like in English...we choose our poems." "In English, we get free writes and I like that." They also talked about strategies that teachers used that students thought were ineffective. "All she does is write on the board and talk..."

What students told me is closely related to what we have learned about student success. Students want to feel that their needs are addressed. A curriculum that is relevant to the students' lives is important to them, and the students want to believe that teachers care for them. A culturally and developmentally responsive learning environment can provide the opportunities for success, and students recognize this.

Challenge

It is clear from the news and the media that schools are evaluated by quantifiable tools. These statistics in turn are used to evaluate and compare schools, teachers, and students. Often, social and economic influences upon these statistics are not considered. Additionally, the appropriateness of the tests is not a topic. If we are to measure success of our schools by the ability of students to work together in an atmosphere of cooperation and peace, we must be committed to developing a learning environment that supports relationships and understanding in addition to changing our curriculum and assessments. Stereotypes must be identified and overcome (Huang 1993). Understanding cultural and gender differences must be a priority and opinions of others must be respected. These actions are "do-able," yet as schools we must work within a society that does not have a clear definition of successful schools.

The challenge then for educators of adolescents is threefold. First they must understand the students' perceptions of success and how these perceptions relate to the norms of the school community. Next, educators must investigate conditions in the school or classroom that may or may not support student success. Finally, educators must provide a learning environment that will support student success in developmentally and culturally appropriate ways.

A student's success is directly related to how the student sees himself or herself as a learner. Thus, the challenges of identity development and success are dual concerns. Another key concern for identity development is the student's relationships within the school community. This challenge will be discussed in the next chapter.

CHAPTER 5

Relationships

Sometimes I'll be thinking of a friend and out of the blue, I'll get a letter or phone call. Now, in the age of technology, I get emails. Or sometimes, when we do get together, it seems that we pick up our conversations right where we left them years before. Friends share something unique. I had a few close friends as a teenager, and even now I have a few special friends. They are ones that I know I can call when I need them or when I have something exciting to share. What defines friendship? What are adolescent friendships? How do friendships fit in middle level schools? What other relationships are crucial in a responsive middle school?

I remember as a child visiting my Aunt Gladys's house. She was a science teacher and always had interesting things around her house. I can remember asking her questions about trees and animals and she seemed to know the answers. I also was amazed when over the summer she had visits from children and teenagers in the small town where she lived. They would come to show her strange insects or fossils that they found in the slate dumped from the coalmines. She always appeared to have time for the young people. Long after she retired, her former students respected and cared about her. How do positive relationships develop between teachers and students?

As an adult I have to develop working relationships with others, some of whom I really wouldn't choose to have as friends. Yet, it was necessary to have professional relationships with them in order to have a smoothly working organization. As students, adolescents must also develop such relationships.

When I was a principal, there was a group of fifth-grade girls who just couldn't seem to get along. Even their mothers got into the melee, and this outside of school situation affected classroom activities. One mother came to see me and insisted that another student be moved from her daughter's group. (She didn't want her daughter moved because she liked the teacher.) When we finally got to the bottom of the situation and the girls had opportunities to face each other in a non-threatening climate, they learned that they could treat each other with respect. How do students learn to work together to promote a positive living and learning environment?

Building relationships takes time and effort. Teachers in developmentally and culturally responsive classrooms take affirmative actions to build positive relationships with their students. Educators influence the opportunities available for students to develop positive relationships by the way they structure their classroom activities to promote interactions among students, by their emphasis on cooperation rather than competition, and by modeling positive relationships. Their productive activities may come naturally as part of their personalities or may have been deliberately chosen and enacted. Teachers cannot control outside influences upon the students in the classroom, nevertheless teachers can set the standards for acceptable behavior within the classroom and model positive relationships.

Furthermore, the biases and assumptions of a teacher may control both the overt and hidden curriculum in the classroom. Teachers have often been called "gatekeepers" as it is the teacher who ultimately chooses what will be taught and how it will be taught in the classroom. Teachers who recognize biases in materials or textbooks that may exacerbate strained relationships discuss the biases critically with their students and engage students in discussions about how such misinformation, or disinformation, may widen the gulf of understanding between students. When teachers examine their own biases in relationships, they can address relationships much more effectively within the classroom.

Relationships within a school environment are multi-dimensional. In a developmentally and culturally diverse middle level school, adolescent issues interact with societal issues to challenge educators. Furthermore, learning environment theory also tells us that positive relationships between adults and students are important in supportive environments (Moos 1991). Students can sense a secure interpersonal environment and also can sense when such an environment does not exist. An understanding of the dynamics of relationships within the system can aid those who are attempting to decipher power and the influences of social constraints upon the learning process. As assumptions about relationships are challenged, students and teachers move from understanding themselves to understanding their relationships with others.

Relationships are often hard to acknowledge and describe because they occur at different levels for different purposes only some of which may be positive. Some may be built on power and result in hegemonic relationships that disenfranchise one group to the betterment of another. When student interactions are influenced by gender, and young women are resigned to take subordinate roles, or those with limited economic resources are prevented from participating in relationship-building activities, the power of some overshadows the roles of others within relationships. Uncovering these relationships exposes contradictions between stated purposes of relationships and the reality of the relationships in the context of school.

Belonging

Being alone. Looking on as others have fun... Listening, listening to them talk about their plans knowing that you will not be included...walking to and from class alone...just to hear someone call from behind...wait, wait for me... Hating to go into the lunchroom knowing that there will be no special table for you to sit at ...waiting at home for someone to call and to sit for hours on the phone ...Trying to make excuses and telling your mother that everything is ok...Being the last to be chosen for teams in gym class and hearing the sneers and groans when a team gets stuck with you... hearing their cruel jokes...trying to pretend I don't hear... Being the one that no one wants to exchange papers with when we were supposed to check each other's papers...Walking home alone with no one to share those special secrets with...Your heart racing when someone does stop to talk to you but finding out they only want to copy your homework...they didn't have time...and knowing that is the only reason they stopped to talk. Looking in...listening...every piece of your body aching to be involved...waiting to be invited but knowing that it will not happen. The teachers try to make you feel special but you know you're not. And then seeing the looks of the special people ...their looks of disgust... or is it pity? ...If only I could get in trouble for passing a note to a friend... what a great trouble...

I can't forget the words of many lonely teens I have encountered in my role as an educator and researcher. Their words lend support to theories about basic relationship needs such as those described by Maslow's hierarchy of needs and William Glasser's Choice Theory. The need to belong has been described as essential for intellectual, social, and emotional growth. William Glasser states that there are five human needs: survival, love and belonging, power, freedom, and fun (1998). It makes sense. Adolescents need to belong; they want to believe that they are respected and cared for in the classroom. Belonging is a major adolescent issue and therefore *not belonging* is also. The plight of the adolescent social outcast, the "isolate" is devastating to those who desperately wish to belong but do not. If an adolescent's basic need for belonging is not fulfilled, achievement or power seems out of his or her reach. Children who tend to be withdrawn or isolated may perceive school as a hostile environment (NWREL 2002).

According to Graham and others (1998), friendship patterns are influenced by socialization outside of school and the related values and beliefs that promote the inclusion or exclusion of individuals within a friendship group. They continued that there are two major elements in friendship development: friendship involves commitment and reciprocity in the relationship; friends view each other as equals. Factors that also influence the development of friendships include opportunities for relationships to develop. If students belong to organizations or participate in the same activities, they are more likely to become friends. When students are able to see similarities with others, the friendship is often bonded by those similarities. Students seem to form groups based upon opportunity for experiences; those who have different background experiences form different groups (O'Neil 1998).

An indication of the adolescent need to belong is the formation of cliques, groups that have exclusive memberships. The criteria for membership in a clique may be activities that provide status. For instance in Eder's study (1995), the cliques were formed around groups of athletes and cheerleaders. Also, in her study, cliques became more defined as students moved to higher grades. Negative effects of cliques on relationships within a classroom may overshadow other associations, and teachers are challenged to diffuse these effects and the power that cliques may have over decision-making and participation.

Group belonging is also an element of the development of a young person's ethnic identity. It is through interactions with others that students can develop a positive or negative image of their own relationships within the school and community. According to John Ogbu and others, some minority students will assume a negative stance toward school success in order to rebel against the dominant group or to fit in with their neighborhood groups (Holcomb-McCoy 1997). If they don't feel acceptance, they may turn to groups that will accept them. In many cases they turn to gangs or to what is often referred to as subcultures. Although youth subcultures are natural in separation of adults and children, feelings of rejection can lead to negative subcultures (Sergiovanni 1994). Adolescents who demonstrate this behavior may do so to defend themselves against rejection and hurt (NWREL 2002).

Group belonging or gang membership can also provide a sense of power to those who feel powerless or alone in an environment that may be interpreted as hostile. "United we stand" is a slogan that is used to suggest political strength and unity that could also be applied to those who are seeking power over the system. Together the group may have a chance for economic success demonstrated by material things—gold jewelry, money—that are symbols of affluence. Also, those who feel powerless in some relationships are able to feel power over others they intimidate. Those who feel oppressed may get satisfaction when they have power over others. Students in a supportive environment realize that differences occur among people and are able to understand the power systems that may determine their acceptance into and rejection from groups. This knowledge may enable those who feel disenfranchised to make choices that will help them reach goals of success and belonging.

Donna Eder's 1995 study of middle school culture gives an inside look into relationships within a middle school. Belonging to a group was important in Eder's study. She found that divisions among students are apparent immediately when one enters a middle school and the one place separate groups are most apparent is in the cafeteria. Furthermore, she found students who did not belong, the isolates, who were not accepted in any group. Therefore, key issues that educators devoted to responsive middle schools address include "How does the need for positive relationships impact upon practices within the school?" and "How do school practices impact upon relationships?"

The constructivist approach holds that social interaction supports learning. Teachers and learners work together to create knowledge. Interactions, both positive and negative, inform the substance of what is learned and the attitude of the learner. By the inherent power of being a teacher, it is the teacher who sets the expectations for relationships within the classroom. Middle level students have formed successful relationships when they can interact with peers and adults showing care, respect, and trust. Thus, perspectives of middle school theory and the influences of race and ethnicity, economic and social class, and gender are critical.

Middle School Perspectives

As students are developing personal identities, the need for relationships with peers increases. As the need to move away from parents develops, young adolescents search for other adults as role models or advisors (Carnegie Council 1989; NASSP 1989; NMSA 1995). Young adolescents experience a need for security and belonging, therefore this need for relationships and security prompts middle school educators to provide a supportive learning environment.

According to Nel Noddings (1992), a caring environment, where caring relationships can thrive and grow, encourages students to develop a caring attitude toward themselves, others, the world, and ideas. Respect, care, and trust are reciprocal. Students need to believe that teachers care for them. Unfortunately, some teachers who do care are not perceived as caring (Beane 1993). It may be a lack of communication or interpretation of what is said. In the students' eyes, words and actions are interpreted through the eyes of adolescents; if one moves from the "typical" perspective, and considers cultural and gender interpretations, the issue becomes more complex. Teachers may act based upon their assumptions about a student and their misinformation may, in fact, alienate the student.

Relationships based on respect and care demand reciprocity between teachers and students. To accomplish this task, educators must create a learning environment that provides opportunities for relationships to develop. Programs and organizational structures may provide the opportunities, but when opportunities become realities individuals invest of themselves. Often it is the adults who are challenged to breach the chasms between people. When teachers observe strained relationships between students in their classrooms, they can try to unravel the problematic situation and provide opportunities for positive interactions. When an atmosphere of trust and care is created, students may also be willing to share of themselves.

Socialization is an important part of intellectual development (NASSP 1989). Opportunities for students to interact positively with their peers include flexible cooperative learning activities. These activities can be progressively designed from simple short pair/share activities to complex problem-based learning projects. The need for students to be involved in small groups for learning is noted. Teams provide opportunities for students to get to know each other well and develop a group identity. Student-teacher teams provide opportunities for teachers to get to know their students well.

Other activities, such as clubs, encourage collaboration and group decision-making and thus provide opportunities for students to develop positive relationship with peers. One school district I know has an after school program during which middle school students and volunteer teachers, administrators, and counselors engage in fun activities. Often, the students are recommended for participation in the activities because of their lack of positive relationships or discipline problems in classrooms. During these activities, students see the adults in a different light; they play and joke together. Students also interact with their schoolmates in supervised activities. Sometimes the recalcitrant students try desperately to hide their enjoyment but ultimately giggle or smile. The program is designed to develop relationships; the students respond and teachers relate that the results of the interactions are observed during the regular school day.

Adults who work in effective middle schools want to be there and have special preparation for working with young adolescents. They are knowledgeable about youth culture. Middle school students tend to be more concerned about the personal attributes than the pedagogical skills of their teachers (George et al. 1992). Attributes in teachers that students believe are important include being a listener, being fair, being flexible and spontaneous, having a sense of humor, and showing respect for students (Davies 1995; George et al. 1992). Students learn about positive relationships when they observe teachers working in collaborative interdisciplinary teams and participating in school governance activities as in site-based management (Carnegie Council 1989).

Advisor/advisee programs provide opportunities for students and teachers to work together in problem solving situations. Students can address personal or group issues. Added to this, advisory programs provide for student needs including the need to feel wanted or to belong, the need for recognition and reward, the need for achievement and success, and the need for fun and adventure (Carnegie 1989; NMSA 1995). Successful implementation of such groups depends on the flexibility and compassion of the teacher (Bergmann and Baxter 1983). Administrative support encourages success of plans to promote positive relationships between teachers and students by providing time and space for the group activities (Shockley, Schumacher, and Smith 1989). Through advisory-type groups, student alienation may be reduced, and students may be provided support and a caring environment (Carnegie Council 1989). Students have an opportunity to express their opinions in non-threatening situations and have their ideas and concerns valued.

Additionally, student participation in programs such as "Adopt a Grandparent" or "Big Buddies" encourage intergenerational relationships (Fand 1996; Beane 1993). Adults who interact with the students and express their interest in the students' talents and interest or acknowledge the service the students provide encourage the development of students' sense of accomplishment. The adults benefit as do the students.

Clearly, middle school theory supports the emphasis on the positive relationships within the learning environment. However, this literature does not adequately address societal factors that influence the development of the relationships. Assumptions and biases of both educators and students intersect with power structures in society to impact on all relationships. Since a constructivist approach assumes that learning occurs in a social-cultural setting, it appears necessary to expand basic middle school discussions to include discussions of gender, social and economic, and racial and ethnic influences of the development of relationships.

Gender Influences

If we close our eyes and reminisce about our elementary days and friends, we will probably find that our friends were very similar to ourselves. Girls had girls for best friends and boys had boys for best friends. In middle schools, same sex friendships are prevalent. This preference for same-sex friendships begins in elementary school and the ways the groups form and behave differ. Girls appear to develop friendships based upon closeness and sharing while boys tend to form groups based upon a common interest or activity. Girls' groups tend to be smaller and more cohesive. Girls tend to look for characteristics that build relationships when choosing friends; boys tend to look for characteristics necessary for status (Manning 1993). Boys' groups tend to be larger and be based upon more aggressive and competitive behaviors. In the elementary years, it is more common for boys to have opportunities to interact with other boys in larger groups; little league baseball or peewee football are supported and promoted in many towns. Some suggest that this social experience contributes to boys' propensity to form larger friendship groups (Graham et al. 1998).

Schools have a powerful influence upon developing relationships and it is at the middle level where many students encounter organizational influences to segregate by sex for the first time A primary vehicle for dividing students is gym class where the boys and girls are separated not only by locker rooms but by the curriculum that is offered. Boys' gym classes often emphasize aggressive, competitive activities while girls' classes do not. If the community has not rallied support for athletic teams prior to the middle school years, young adolescents begin the segregation process when schools promote athletic teams and cheerleading groups to support the teams. Boys are the stars and girls are their admirers.

Relationships based on gender have been well documented, especially in the work of Sadker and Sadker (1994). Not only are organizational structures responsible for some differences but biases or attitudes of teachers can have dramatic effects. Teacher influences on gender relationships are at times subtle and at other times overt. Eder (1995) tells of coaches who referred to the boys who were not athletic with derogatory words often related to being like girls. These coaches and gym teachers urged athletes to be mean and aggressive. Boys were encouraged to be tough and competitive and be insensitive to the feelings of others. It was common to refer to boys who did not act in masculine manners in terms that hinted that the young boys may be homosexual. At an early age, young boys and girls are taught to use harassment as a means of control. Such an institutionalization of gender related power structures occur in society as well (Talbot 2002). Schools that accept negative behaviors legitimize them.

Teachers' actions can be much more subtle and institutionalized. When we have students line up by boys and girls, or we pit boys against girls in competitive activities in the classroom, artificial boundaries are created which may influence and support gender stereotypes and relationships. Often, in elementary school classrooms, tables are designated as boys' tables and girls' tables; playground areas are assigned based on boys' areas and girls' areas (Thorne 1992). These institutionalized divisions can become internalized and accepted as natural by the students.

Gender issues may also be impacted by instructional strategies. Sometimes cooperative learning groups, which literature suggests develop relationships, may actually inhibit the development of leadership skills in girls. It has been found that girls will hesitate to take leadership roles or speak out in classrooms rather than upset relationship dynamics within the classroom (Buck 2002). For this reason, some educators propose same-sex cooperative learning groups or even same-sex classrooms. Competitive activities may also limit girls' achievement. Often girls will be reluctant to stand out because they may not want to look "too smart" or they may not want to win if it means someone else will lose.

Developmentally, appearance is an issue for young adolescents. If we look at movies, television, and magazines directed at teens, the message is clear. Makeup, diets, clothing, and jewelry are marketed to make girls popular or "sexy." Having the economic resources to meet these appearance standards may be a real obstacle for some young adolescents and may not be for others. Appearance may determine the level of confidence that adolescents have when they want to belong. Appearance may also be criteria that adolescents use to include or exclude others from their groups. In Eder's 1995 study, peer interactions seemed to focus on how one looked ranging from weight to clothes that were worn. Those who were considered unattractive were often the recipient of insults and were either isolates or in low-status groups.

Boy-girl relationships are beginning to emerge during the young adolescent years. Adults often refer to these relationships as crushes or "puppy love," but the relationships are important to the young people. I can remember being in junior high and worrying about who would ask me to dance at the sock hop or to sit with them on the bus to basketball games. I remember the first boy that had a "crush" on me and gave me a gift. During the late elementary years, the relationships may start as teasing or chasing games. By middle school, boys and girls may enter in dating or pseudo-dating relationships that may change several times throughout a school year. For girls, having a steady boyfriend often indicates their attractiveness or social status. In the eyes of other girls, having a *boyfriend* elevates the status of girls; however, the status of boys with their peers does not seem to be affected when they have steady *girlfriends* (Thorne 1992). Dating and sexual activity are becoming more prevalent among young adolescents. It is not uncommon for sexual activity to begin during the middle school years. As Margaret Mead proposed, because of secular trend, behaviors that have been associated with older groups are found in younger groups in each generation. As adults we may be uncomfortable with the new mores of young adolescents; however, we must acknowledge the situation.

The socialization of gendered power begins at an early age and by the middle school years the roles have become habit. The feminine ethos of caring may in fact be a negative influence on girls' relationships as in their willingness and effort to care for others they may take upon a subservient role in relationships. Additionally, cultural expectations around gender roles contribute to the role of girls and boys in relationships. Media and subtle messages presented to girls during the impressionable young adolescent stage help reinforce such attitudes about relationships. Boys are given the message that relationships are not to be taken seriously, that girls are toys to be discarded when they are no longer attractive or useful. Without critically examining the gender, social, and economic influences, the impact of power relationships perpetuates the inequalities.

Racial and Ethnic Influences

Friendships are often complicated by racial diversity. In high school, my brothers and I had friends that were of different races and religions than we were. However, as I think back, we were school friends and even belonged to some organizations together, but we didn't have quite the same relationships with these friends as we did with other friends. I didn't question the situation then. That's just the way things were. The understanding of racial differences begins in early childhood. In young children, choosing a best friend from a person's same race is rather common. However, as children grow older, African American students are less likely to choose Euro-Americans as best friend during adolescence; however, even though they do not choose Euro Americans as best friends, they still maintain more overall friendliness toward same-race and cross-race friends than do Euro-Americans (Graham et al. 1998).

Race and gender have been found to be factors in developing friendships, although gender does seem to be a greater determiner of friendship than race (Graham et al. 1998). Boys seemed to have more same sex/cross race friendships as they got older. However, this difference may be the result of differences in friendship patterns in girls and boys. Girls seem to be more exclusive in their friendships. Also boys have more opportunities than girls to include students of other races in their friendship circles, particularly through sports teams.

Classrooms that have more balanced diversity provide more opportunities for cross-race friendships (Graham et al. 1998). Adolescents attending integrated schools have generally reported having close interethnic (racial) friendships; however, they have also reported not seeing their interethnic friends outside of school as frequently as they saw their same-race friends (Branch 2001). It appears that over time, cross-race friendships have been more accepted, but the preference still remains for same-race friendships (Graham et al. 1998). This may, however, be a function of the neighborhoods within which the students live.

Although relationships between students are formidable in their lives, relationships formed with teachers are also significant. Studies have shown that distinct differences in the ways teachers and students relate in the classroom can be identified. Irvine (1986) reports that black students have less favorable interactions with their teachers than do white students. Curiously, different relationships have been found even when the teachers themselves have been Black. Black girls have significantly less positive interactions with their teachers and are given fewer opportunities to answer or speak up in class than others beginning in the upper elementary grades. Irvine also found that white teachers have more verbal interactions, including praise and criticism, and more nonverbal praise toward boys than girls. His observation is consistent with other gender research. However, Irvine additionally found that black boys receive more nonverbal criticism than black girls, white girls, and white boys.

One key element in relationships, especially at the middle school level, is trust. Students want to trust their friends and their teachers. Trust may be missing especially in relationships between white teachers and their diverse students. Cultural mistrust of white teachers is often found among black students. In a study of 1,328 sixth and seventh grade boys, approximately one third of the boys mistrusted Whites and white teachers. Foreign-born Haitians showed the most mistrust while the lowest level of mistrust was found among boys from the Caribbean Islands (Osher and Mejia 1999). This same phenomenon is found among Native Americans. The mistrust may lead to misunderstandings about education and the teachers within the system. Inner-city Native American youth, who feel mistrustful of their schools, are often drawn to gangs in order to find connections with their culture. Lack of connectedness is related to high absenteeism and dropout rates among many Native American students (Cleary and Peacock 1998).

Mistrust based on cultural or racial backgrounds comes from a history of oppression and is imbedded in cultural tradition. Social, economic, and political influences have influenced the way that those of many cultures look upon white educators. Cleary and Peacock (1999) emphasize that an effective teacher is a learner in the school community. They indicate that tasks for a teacher include developing trust and a culturally relevant curriculum. Strategies they recommend include connecting with the community and developing culturally relevant curriculum. They also recommend developing relationships with students and using activities and cooperative learning. These strategies and other strategies Cleary and Peacock recommend for teaching Native American students are in accord with middle level theory. In a culturally and responsive middle level school, a culturally relevant curriculum can demonstrate that a teacher cares about the students and may develop trust.

Osher and Mejia (1999) suggest that there are four barriers to cultural integration and the development of relationships within the school community. They suggest that those in the community often do not see how their own cultural beliefs and values influence their interactions with others. When teachers of diverse students do not recognize the inherent inconsistencies between their own background experiences and those of their students, misunderstandings and mistrust may result. The authors also suggest a barrier exists when the leaders or those who hold power in the organization don't represent the community. If students only see white, male principals, the students may believe that they do not have access to decision-making or power. Current events in society that exacerbate cultural difference may flow into the school setting. This has been especially apparent in our current political climate where mistrust of those who may be of Middle Eastern descent is rampant. Furthermore, when racial profiling or high-profile minority court cases are headlines, society's insecurities are translated into strained relationships within the school community. Finally, there is a tendency for one oppressed group to believe that the situation is worse for them than it is for others. This is especially possible within the young adolescent experience because adolescents are concerned about their place and relationships within their peer groups.

It is clear that the sense of belonging is a factor in schools and students who may have racial or ethnic differences may feel like outsiders. When minority students perceive that they are part of the school community and not inferior to the dominant group, they do not experience school failure as much. At times, success depends upon the desire to assimilate into the dominant group (Peña 1997). Nevertheless, those students who successfully assimilate into the dominant group may in turn be alienated from others of their own race. They are accused of "acting white" or being traitors to their own culture. Often peer and family pressures discourage assimilation, and the students are caught in a stressful and often lonely position.

Socio-economic Influences

Since friendships are often determined by outside influences, separation of people is a function of social and economic influences. When young adolescents are limited by finances and excluded from activities because they cannot afford to participate, their access to situations that create opportunities for friendships is also limited. Eder (1995) found that social class had an influence on grouping. Students in her study used special terms for students in lower social classes just as Eckert reported in her book, *Jocks and Burnouts* (1989). The students in the higher-status groups spoke of students in the lower-status groups with negative terms and many times the terms related to appearance. In the 1970s, TV viewers the sitcom, *Welcome Back Kotter,* immortalized the "sweathogs," a classroom filled with misfits. Conversely, students in more affluent groups are often given names based on their preppy clothes.

In many of these situations, the students who were in the lower-class groups thought the students in the higher-class groups were "stuck-up'" and the students in the higher groups thought the students in the lower aggressive or untrustworthy. Each group appeared to want to avoid members of the other group. In many studies, there were at least two distinct groups and also students who were on the fringes of groups. Some students tried to emulate the dress of specific groups in order to be accepted. The lowest status of all was held by the isolates, and many times appearance was often a focus of their exclusion.

Not long ago I had students in my educational foundations course look at their old yearbooks. One of their tasks was to look at how many times their pictures appeared and to reflect upon their findings. For many adolescents, visibility in the school is equated with popularity. Donna Eder found that popularity was equated with visibility in activities such as cheerleading, athletics, or student government in the middle school that she studied. The key to popularity was being known by many people but not necessarily liked by many people. She also observed that most of those in the low status group, the ones that were not popular, were from working-class or rural families (1995).

The ability to be visible by participating in extracurricular activities such as cheerleading is a function of economics. Often low-income students are not able to buy supplies or have transportation that is necessary for participation. Sometimes, attending practices requires parents to provide transportation to or from practices, and work schedules make that difficult or impossible. Students may not have the funds to take music, dance, or gymnastic lessons. Additionally, rural students who are also low-income are particularly affected by a lack of transportation.

Brantlinger (1993) suggests that adolescents' images of others often are a result of social class. Part of the impression is because of the clothes that groups of students choose to wear. Students from higher income groups often believe that students from low income groups are violent or aggressive because of that group's tendency to assume an identity symbolized by black or leather-looking clothes decorated with chains or metal. Brantlinger also proposes that the low-income students purposefully send messages about aggressiveness and power to onlookers. They believe that others believe they are inferior and powerless and they want to demonstrate power.

The interaction of gender and socio-economic influences is especially problematic. Working-class and lower income girls are especially influenced by societal messages about relationships. For many, the cycle of poverty suggests to young adolescent girls that their role in relationships is that of the supportive persons, not the leaders. Positive relationships seem to have a more direct effect on disadvantaged students' achievement (Braddock and McFarland 1993). When the influences of economics, gender, and racial, or ethnic situations determine relationship dynamics within a classroom, the challenge for teachers to create a supportive environment for all students is unavoidable.

What Do Students Have to Say?

Students in my research groups suggested that when teachers help them it is an indicator of friendliness and care. For instance, one student said that a friendly teacher is one who "will actually talk to you or help you with your work." The idea that helping is an indicator of friendliness and care is not unique to the students I interviewed. Students must feel that teachers want to help; that teachers understand their questions and frustrations. Schools can create this atmosphere of help and caring in the classroom and if the school and teachers will ask themselves such question as "Am I using put-downs with students who need extra help?" or "How can I encourage students to come to me for help with their work?" In some schools, teachers have office hours much like college professors. Other schools provide after-school tutoring sessions; still others have tutorial periods built into the school day. There is no prescription. A school must look at its needs and resources to find feasible options.

Students want teachers to respect their feelings. Students in my study gave specific examples where they believed that teachers did not respect their feelings.

> Like if you and your friend were in this big fight and you really can't concentrate on your work because you were in this fight They expect you to do all this stuff... prompt and neat and stuff...and all that and you just can't if you've been fighting with your friends... Your mind's just not on it.

Furthermore, the students in my study perceived their teachers as strict, but many of the examples they gave had to do with relationships with their friends. They felt that friendships override rules that they believed were unreasonable.

> You can't go up and give your best friend a hug. It doesn't matter whether it is a girl or a guy. You just can't.
>
> If we want to just link arms, they come up and say, "No, no. You can't do that. You're not allowed to link arms in school."
>
> When one of my friends, she was crying I just went up to her and hugged her.
>
> Stuff like that, I do it anyway. I just don't care 'cause my friend is more important to me, I guess.

Trust is an important aspect of relationships between teachers and students. Some of the students believed that their teachers didn't trust them and they didn't trust their teachers.

> If there is a fight in the hall or something and you are right there, they suspect you are in it and they won't listen to your side. Even if you were...say that you were just walking by when it happened. They think you did something.

> They think you are an accomplice, too.

> I'd probably talk to my friends. Well, maybe I'd go [to the guidance office] sometimes. It depends on the situation 'cause they might tell my mom and stuff.

> I don't talk to [school personnel]. I can tell my mom anything and she won't get mad. Well, she'll get mad, but she will understand. She knows she was a kid once and stuff she did. She'd just tell me she was disappointed in me.

Students may feel that their needs and issues are of value when they have the opportunity to participate in the decision-making process within the school. Rules clearly are an issue. In Chapter 2, the connection between relationship and citizenship was established. Chapter 6, Community, explores the role of student participation in school decisions and the development of trust in such relationships.

Challenge

Middle schools are challenged to provide opportunities for the students to develop positive relationships with their peers, in addition to adults. Studies have shown that adolescents only spend up to 7% of their day exclusively with adults (Berger 1991). It is through positive relationships with peers that young adolescents may successfully transition into adulthood as they move away from dependence on parents. As this happens, the ideas and values of the peer group become increasingly influential (Ausubel 1968; Berger 1991). The Carnegie Council (1989) suggests that schools be organized in a manner that provides opportunities for students to interact with their peers in positive ways.

Opportunities for interactions may be limited by lock-step scheduling which regulates both student and teacher time within the school day. Flexible scheduling, which incorporates such activities as advisory time, supports the development of relationships. Additionally, exploratory courses, such as studying a language, cooking, or river pollution during which students and teachers investigate concerns together, promote sharing of ideas and values, and can encourage relationships.

It is not hard to pay attention to students and their interests, though those who have achieved the goal feel it means a few less visits to the faculty room or a few more evenings back at school. Successful schools have teachers who find time to interact with students inside and outside the classroom. Teachers and adults must ask themselves "What do I know about the interests of the students in my classroom or my school?" The NMSA (1995) recommends that every student have an adult who knows him or her well. Knowing the interests of students can open lines of communication; classroom lessons and activities can surely revolve around topics of interest to the students. Teachers may learn about their students' interests and values by talking with the students. Communication with students is visited in Chapter 7, Dialogues. When dialogues occur, students will feel their interests are, if not shared, at least respected by others.

Not only is it important for people within the school to promote a positive climate, the NMSA suggests that a middle school building should reflect a positive school climate also (1995). In his book, *Savage Inequalities*, Jonathan Kozol suggests that the inadequate and dilapidated school buildings that many students in our country attend impart a message that students are not valued or not recipients of the care of society (1991). Still, conditions have not changed for many children. Lynn Estomin, in her 2002 video, *No Justice, No Peace,* shows schools in Cincinnati with ceilings draped with tarps to keep plaster from falling on students. The students, and those who care about them, believe that justice escapes them.

The challenge of developing positive relationships cannot be divorced from other challenges for middle level education, especially the challenges of Identity Development and Citizenship. Young adolescents must see themselves as members of families, school, and community and as friends. As students participate in school and community, relationships evolve. If students do not see themselves as members of families, school, and community the challenge of Citizenship can be even more difficult.

CHAPTER 6

Community

I must admit, that teaching science wasn't one of my favorite things to do. I was one of those students who didn't like science. One year our middle school decided to have two-person teams for the fifth graders and I was asked if I would like to switch to fifth grade and teach two subjects. I said I would be willing to teach math and any subject but science. Guess what! Since science and math are traditionally grouped together, I taught science and math. I was given a "process approach" kit and sent on my way. I found out that science wasn't too bad after all and I actually had fun with the materials in the kit.

Later, in another school district where I had to teach science without a supporting teacher kit, I decided to design units based upon what the students and I wanted to know. (This was before the day of "inquiry-based" science.) I was supposed to teach a unit about animals, but I had freedom to make some choices. I didn't know much about animals, but I remembered that my two sons liked to look at the birds that came to our birdfeeder. Birds became the focus of the unit.

The first thing I did was to fill my room with pictures and displays about birds. I covered every available space. I displayed some intriguing books, pictures, and even cartoons so prominently that students couldn't miss them. I caught the students looking at all the things, but the trick was that I didn't mention anything about birds for a week or so before I began the unit. Then when I told the students we were going to study birds, I asked the students to pose "twenty questions" that they would like to have answered. The students included higher-order questions on the list: "Why do...? What happens if...? How does...?" They even asked questions for which I did not know the answers. We wrote the questions on a big chart and I told them that I would help them find the answers but they could bring answers to the class. Even some of the most recalcitrant students got involved. They brought magazine or newspaper articles to school; they found books in the library; they even used the *Guinness Book of World Records* to share unique or curious facts. As we found answers to their questions, we would check them off on our chart. The students were thrilled when the list of remaining questions got smaller. When I taught a lesson, I told the student which of their questions I was addressing. Without official "standards," these students achieved a high level of thinking and learning. We answered all their questions and even more. The students had ownership of their learning; they observed me teaching to their interests; we learned together.

When I first began studying middle school environments and student perceptions, I chose the term citizenship to describe one of the challenges for middle school education. I proposed that the challenge of Citizenship was to provide opportunities for students to make decisions about their learning activities and to address social issues by understanding the consequences of behaviors, by problem solving, and by being active participants in the school community. Imbedded in my definition are the key elements of citizenship: freedom of choice, respect for others, understanding one's own opinions while realizing other opinions may differ, and fairness.

Recently, I decided that the word *citizenship* really doesn't convey the meaning I want. Individuals bring to words their own backgrounds and experiences. Events in the United States and the world have entangled the flag, unquestioning allegiance to country, and politics into the definition of citizenship. Talk show pundits debate the meaning of citizenship and right-wing and left-wing politicians have chosen to polarize the debates. For these reasons, I have decided not to use the word citizenship to describe a challenge for middle level education in this chapter; instead I will use the term *community*. Moreover, in my paradigm, *democracy* is a key term in the understanding of citizenship and community. In democratic schools, students have a set of beliefs based upon principles of equal opportunities for participation and a set of values that protect the individual rights of all students while recognizing the right to disagree. A democratic, supportive learning community encourages student success, and it provides a learning experience that may translate into positive participation in society.

The connection between democracy and education is not new. When Dewey is mentioned in educational foundations books, he is labeled a proponent of *progressive education*, but the democracy connection often is not made clear. Dewey proposed that students should learn about the process of democracy by practicing democracy throughout their educational experiences (1916). By not permitting students to practice democratic practices, students are conditioned to become comfortable in a hierarchical power system which disenfranchises some members of the society, thus creating tension between the democratic ideals professed by schools and the reality of lived experience (Shor 1992). Middle school researchers Lounsbury and Clark (1990) found that students have been conditioned for passivity so they don't even consider that they could be part of the decision-making process. A constructivist paradigm implies a community of learners where students and teachers engage in dialogue to create opportunities for learning (Sergiovanni 1996) and where knowledge is created by collaboration not competition (Jonassen 1994). This dialogue encourages students to use levels of thinking beyond mere memorization of facts about democracy and community; students are encouraged to question, to speculate, to analyze, and to evaluate. Students are encouraged to stretch beyond current situations and create solutions to problems. Thus, administrators, teachers, and students work together to create the conditions for learning. Shared ideals give meaning to school life by answering these questions: "What is this school about? What is our image of role of learners in school decision-making? How do we work together as colleagues?" (Sergiovanni 1992, 41)

Middle School Perspectives

According to the National Middle School Association (1995), young adolescents wish to belong to a group. They are generally idealistic, socially conscious, and desire to make the world a better place, often by participating in real-life problem solving activities. Middle school educators are charged to provide a learning environment in which opportunities exist for authentic participation. This process is most observable by the student at the classroom level; the attitudes of the teachers, and their assumptions about the abilities of their students, determine the extent to which participation will occur. In a developmentally responsive middle school classroom, students learn to be problem solvers and understand consequences of their behavior. However, as students look to adults as role models, they may also pay attention to flaws or inconsistencies between what they see in society and the values espoused by adults.

An authentic school community considers the students to be "experts' about themselves and youth culture. Students need to believe they are participants in a school system that is responsive to their needs and in a situation where they have clear rights and responsibilities (Carnegie Council 1989). Students in a supportive learning environment do not take passive roles in the production of knowledge but help create meaning for the experiences in school (Apple and Beane 1995).

The Carnegie Council recommends that a middle school be a "community for learning" (1989, 37). The National Middle School Association proposes that all stakeholders should be involved in a shared vision. The task of creating a community of learners suggests these questions: What is a community of learners? How does the ethos of community relate to middle school philosophy? How are the learning environment, the school community, and the students' construction of knowledge related?

Roles in the Community

The primary groups of school community members are the teachers, administrators, and students. Roles of the members are defined by the paradigms of knowledge, the belief systems, the values, and the power hierarchies within the school. According to the Carnegie Council on Adolescent Development (1989), decision-making possibilities of members of the school community have been limited, often by outside political or social pressures and other times by the power hierarchies within the school system itself. Therefore, administrators and teachers must have greater control of their professional actions and students must be able to observe their teachers participating in the decision-making process.

In the constructivist approach to teaching and learning, teachers are empowered learners (Cannon 1995). In a middle school that strives to be a community of learners, administrators share the decision making with teachers and students (Carnegie Council 1989) and the strengths of members of the community are acknowledged and used to benefit all (Sergiovanni 1996). Each member of a community is able to maintain individuality while at the same time being willing to be a member of a group—a challenge to all (Nodding 1992; Sergiovanni 1996). By building on diversity, the school community is enriched.

Maxwell and Thomas (1991) and Sergiovanni (1992) suggest that the power framework in the school determines the learning atmosphere; i.e., whether the school considers itself an organization or a community. In organizations, power hierarchies are top-down, with principals given authority and supposed expertise because of position or rank. This top-down arrangement is then translated in the classrooms that are dominated by teacher-talk and the belief that a defined body of knowledge exists and must be transmitted to the students. Such an orientation is exemplified in Tyler's rationale that emphasizes deliberate organization of content material for continuity, sequence, and organization. Structure of courses and planning for instruction are selected, organized, and evaluated (Tyler 1949).

In a community, as opposed to an organization, decision-making is shared and strengths and abilities of all members are recognized. Students, as well as teachers and administrators, participate in decisions about learning strategies and areas of inquiry.(1990) suggests that those who feel they have a voice in the decision-making exhibit greater commitment to the decision and are willing to take responsibility. When those in the school do not have a chance to participate, no one takes responsibility, blame is directed externally, and adversarial relationships become a feature of school life. Thus, the student-teacher relationship is critical in the school environment (NMSA 1995; Strodl 1997). As middle schools attempt to establish a school environment that supports learning, it is imperative that the perceptions of students be included in the review of the environment.

A school environment that promotes the development of community tends to model community throughout. Administrators nurture the atmosphere of community by empowering teachers and involving them in decision-making. This in turn models cooperative behavior to students. Interdisciplinary teams, comprised of teachers and students, require collaboration and negotiation, form meaningful decisions, and promote responsibility for actions (Beane 1993; Carnegie Council 1989). Teamwork provides situations that encourage students to understand the relationship between power and responsibility (Apple and Beane 1995).

Kaba (2001) reports that four reasons have been identified for student participation in school decision-making. The first is based upon the concept of a free, democratic society and those affected have a right to voice their ideas. Second, students who participate have a sense of ownership and involvement in the school. When they participate in decision-making, they are provided with education for democracy and citizenship. Finally, when students are involved in making decisions, the decisions have credibility with the student body. Students exhibit community when they participate meaningfully in school and community. To be contributing members, students need to address social issues by understanding the consequences of behaviors, by problem solving, and using interpersonal skills. Students in a culturally responsive middle school appreciate diverse cultures and embrace the concept of human dignity. Democratic principles should be evident throughout the school and curriculum (Beane 1993) to support young adolescents striving to become independent first from family then from other adults and who are anxious to make decisions.

Relationships and meaningful participation are supported when the adults within the school and classroom environments provide opportunities for students to practice decision-making skills. One way teachers can help students develop decision-making skills is by inviting students to make choices about units of study designed around students' concerns including questions posed by students. When the curriculum is based on interests and needs of the students, and is culturally relevant, the school experience is more meaningful. Once students observe their ideas and opinions being respected, they may be more willing to contribute in other situations. As teachers model their respect, students may be more willing to respect the ideas of others. Teachers' actions demonstrate the way that the learning environment encourages students to be active or passive learners.

Decision sharing experiences can and do exist. I know of one middle school where students interviewed the candidates for their new principal. Students, in a group, met with candidates, asked questions, evaluated the answers, and voiced their opinions to the school board. The successful candidate told me that the students' questions were the hardest and most perceptive during the interview process. The students who represented their peers felt their opinions and ideas were valued. They had ownership in the decision.

Barnes (1996) suggests that hindrances exist in the development of relationships between children and adults. Communication may be blocked not only by the unequal powers within the relationship, but also by students' assumptions about how a person of the professional's gender or culture should act. I used to laugh when my students, who were used to seeing me in my "principal suits," would act surprised at seeing me on Saturdays in the local discount stores wearing paint spattered sweats. They thought it was great when

I wore sneakers to school with my suits. (They didn't know that I had hurt my foot and was under doctor's orders to wear the shoes!) Educators make themselves seem real to the students when they share a little of themselves such as family pictures or stories about pets. When teachers trust their students with a little of the teachers' lives, students may be willing to trust the teachers with stories of their own.

According to systems theory, a classroom is part of a larger system, the school that is also part of even a larger system, the district. The district is part of the larger community. Since classrooms are part of a larger system, they are necessarily influenced by outside factors. The classroom itself is a system that responds to internal factors. Furthermore, it is in the classroom where students have the most intimate school experiences. When teachers and students develop positive interpersonal relationships within the classroom, a community of learners can exist. As students' skills grow, the outside of school community becomes a site for student participation and student interests, and concerns can be addressed in a wider context. Community organizations provide resources and personnel for in-school activities as well as sites for learning experiences out of school. For example, service projects enable students to demonstrate the community skills they have developed. Thus, the community becomes a classroom and students engage in relationships that build on communication and caring. This service can be part of the required curriculum but that tends to cause controversy. Students who see the need for projects, plan the projects, and see the results of their efforts benefit from the experience. According to the National Middle School Association (1995), young adolescents are beginning to be concerned about social issues and real-life situations.

Building community cannot develop without the qualities of trust, respect, and care. A feminist pedagogy supports a learning community in which participants share knowledge and share the power to determine the conditions that support the production of knowledge (Brady 1995). An atmosphere of trust and respect facilitates open discourse within which students and teachers share ideals and beliefs, though without understanding invisible ideologies, this knowledge does not become emancipatory (Taylor et al. 1995). According to Nel Noddings (1992), as teachers become empowered and actively involved in the learning community, students become empowered. In fact, students often have important insights into what works and doesn't work. As teachers feel secure and confident in their own professionalism, student judgments and opinions are received constructively rather than negatively.

Students demonstrate their participation in classroom activities when they give opinions and ask questions (Fraser 1990). Tensions may arise within the learning environment when students are encouraged to take active roles in the construction of knowledge. Power issues revolving around student and teacher roles and control of the classroom may emerge (Strodl 1997). The value put on student opinions is related to the community orientation within the environment (Carnegie Council 1989; Williamson and Johnston 1996). Students working in cooperative groups have opportunities to collaborate in problem solving. Group projects within the school setting, whether part of academic subject area studies or student interest area activities, afford a means for group interactions. Heterogeneous groups made up of students with varying abilities and interests provide students with life-like situations where students can benefit from social and intellectual interactions of a diverse population (Carnegie Council 1989; NASSP 1989; NMSA 1995).

Feminist theory is concerned that the illusion of student autonomy and control may supplant authentic participation. Power within the classroom may be mediated by gender or racial relationships; the interpretations that students and teachers make of relationships are not the same for all the interpreters. Teachers' outlooks or preconceived images of the students they teach can limit the development of authentic relationships (Anyon 1995; Gresson 1997). Some teachers may have negative expectations of students and be afraid of allowing students to participate in decisions (Gersch 1996; Smith 1995). Community theory cautions against the "engineered consent" and pseudo-participation that can occur without careful deliberate inclusion of students in discussions and decision-making (Beane 1992, 35). Constructivist learning theory suggests that a synergistic relationship exists between learning and control. As students make decisions about their learning, identify needs and wants, and make decisions about the learning environment which would make the learning environment conducive to the attainment of their wants and needs, the ability to be active and contributing community members develops (Apple and Beane 1995; Kohn 1996).

Cultural Influences

Culture wars in our own society have placed schools at the center of controversy. An accepted purpose of schools has been to transmit the values and beliefs of a society. This is where the problem arises in a pluralistic society.

Whose beliefs and values should the school promote? In a democratic society, the values of all stakeholders should have attention. Within these multiple perspectives, the goal for a developmentally and culturally responsive school is to find common ground and common values that all can accept. The ways our diverse school communities meet this goal will vary as no one program meets the needs of every school. Furthermore, as the school population changes, schools must adapt and change. School should model democracy in order to teach democracy.

Sergiovanni (1996) states that according to the constructivist paradigm, knowledge is considered both individually and communally owned. By understanding the constraints of their own oppressions, the disenfranchised understand their own power as knowers (Weiler 1991). The production of knowledge is shared. When students are able to understand circumstances and conditions in personal context as well as consider the knowledge in light of the perspectives of others, real learning occurs (Sergiovanni 1996). A learning environment that encourages participation and respect for self and other could encourage such understandings. When students have an opportunity to discover inconsistencies in arguments or misinformation that has been provided in their texts, to learn how the texts were developed, they can better understand the effect of their learning on the decisions that they make.

Acceptance or rejection of students within a school community may be defined by culture or gender. Furthermore, the participation roles of students have often been defined by students' culture or gender. A prime example is the expectation that girls do not play football. However, just recently it was announced that a girl is playing on a Division I college football team as a place kicker. Even teachers and administrators succumb to gender messages unwittingly. During meetings, note taking is often delegated to women, and women obligingly take notes. I sat in meetings when I was one of the few females in attendance. There were puzzled looks when I asked men to take the notes or when I was asked to take notes, I pushed the pen and tablet to men. The assumption that many hold is that being "secretary" is women's work. Teachers must be aware of the messages being sent to students about the value of their participation and opinions (Nieto 1994). Teachers' comments and gestures give messages about whether they approve of a student's value or participation in an activity.

Tensions may also be present when students raise sensitive issues about gender or culture in discussions, especially when those issues are in conflict with the dominant culture, which in effect silences those views. This in essence legitimizes racism, discriminations, or other related topics (Nieto 1994). The choices made as to which voices are legitimized and which voices are not is a political statement about the values and beliefs to be honored. Schools that have groups that are segregated by race tend to have students who do not feel connected to the school. Extracurricular activities that connect students to the school community have been shown to increase connectedness with school and relates to academic achievement (McNeely et al. 2002). Middle school ideals suggest that opportunities for all students to participate be maximized instead of having a few select extracurricular activities; intramural teams or clubs that serve the majority of the students should be emphasized. If students do not feel connected interpersonally or by curriculum, their ties to the school are limited. By neglecting the history and culture of some, the empowerment of all students is threatened (Shor 1992).

A caring school environment cannot cure all the ills of society; cultural issues such as unemployment and low income are not cured in a school setting. Nevertheless, caring relationships between adults and students and a feeling of connectedness in the school community have been found to have a positive effect upon the students (Resnick, Harris, and Blum 1993). The "family values" position is that young people need to be connected to their family; this argument certainly has merit. Nevertheless, young adolescents need to be connected to others outside their family as one of the tasks of adolescents is to move away from the family into society.

One cultural difference that has not been included in the discussions so far is a position that does not support the concepts of community and consensus. The problem arises when teachers, who are trying to be inclusive, are confronted with those whose values do not support inclusivity. According to literature provided by such groups, they believe that coming to a consensus requires that students give up their values of faith. Instead of students being able to question, they are expected to blindly accept the beliefs of their parents and not respect the rights of others to have different beliefs. One example of the impact of the controversy is the debate over the Newberry Award winning book for young adolescents, *The Giver* (Associated Press 2001).

In the story of *The Giver* (Lowery 1993), young children are raised communally and are taught to follow community rules. Society is managed and families are controlled. At the end of the story, the young hero questions the rules and rebels against conformity. The book deals with issues of euthanasia, service to the community, and sharing feelings—ideas with which many disagree, therefore, they believe the book should not be discussed in school at all. It forces "children to think the unthinkable and reconsider the values they learned at home" (Kjos 1996). That may be the problem; children are asked to think!

Kjos (1996) challenges the use of community service and suggests there is a hidden agenda for schools that are trying to control the minds of students. This position suggests that when students are guided in their reflections, teachers are trying to superimpose their beliefs upon the innocent minds of children. Those like Kjos who oppose *The Giver* propose that such activities such as guided reflection are anti-Christian. Community experiences are called indoctrination; teachers are accused of bringing globalist and occult ideas into the classroom. Kjos says that Bloom's taxonomy subverts Christian values. Thus, those who disagree with Kjos's perspective are subversive and should not be trusted. Others are supposed to respect her opinion but others' opinions are not to be respected. When teachers discuss sharing, they are accused of being anti-American. Those who profess to be supportive of a free country believe that they are the only ones who are free to have beliefs and that students should not be able to learn about other beliefs. Smacks of repressive societies that they profess to abhor. In their eyes, citizenship is based upon unquestioning allegiance to beliefs.

Using fear of a *New World Order* (Robertson 1991), organizations and politicians they support suggest that schools be privatized by 2010 to protect children against the evils of society as they see them. Other groups do not want their children to study psychology, sociology, or anthropology. They propose that the important people in the history of our country have been Christians and those who do not follow the ways that the group promotes are ruining our country (Citizens for Excellence in Education 2003). These ideas certainly should alarm citizens of the United States who are Christian, Jewish, atheist, or whatever. These groups do not seem to recognize that we are in a global society whether we want to be or not. Nationalism, without an understanding of how our nation fits into the world, will not insure survival of our nation. In a democratic country, supposedly based upon the premise of separation of church and state, schools are agents of society; what values do we as a society hold?

All stakeholders, in a responsive school, have a voice in decision-making. How do we deal with those whose culture does not want the children to learn about evolution, or Harry Potter, or other religions? In California, schools were accused of brainwashing seventh graders when they learned about Islam in their social studies classes even when the state curriculum standards include a requirement to "analyze the geographic, political, economic, religious, and social structures of the civilization of Islam in the Middle Ages" (California Department of Education 2003). The state standards also require studies of China and Europe during the same time period. According to some groups, the only religion students should learn about is Christianity. Kjos (1996) suggests that schools should know the *facts* about Columbus and not study the implication of Columbus's arrival in the New World. In other words, curriculum should only discuss the facts as they have been taught instead of encouraging students to uncover the multiple perspectives of events in history.

In a public school system, in a democracy, which provides universal education, how can one group of stakeholders control what is taught and how it is taught? How do schools work with groups who do not believe in coming to consensus? Schools, as institutions within a democratic society are challenged to encourage students to have care, respect and trust as basic core values. These schools have a shared set of norms and values. Coming to consensus means to agree on commonalities while respecting the rights of others to have their own beliefs. How does this work with a group that sees only one way and other views are subversive, demonic or from the occult? Such groups seek to remove from the curriculum anything that is different from their beliefs. The Carnegie Council report *Turning Points: Preparing American Youth for the 21st Century* is attacked because it recommends community service for youth. The opposing group proposes that the experiences are designed by sociologists to give Anti-Christian perspectives. Our society and our country are challenged as we are working with young adolescents. What is the role of the school? Whose values are to be considered? How do we honor those who are different? How can we profess the ideal of our beliefs while suppressing such a view? Yet, if we follow such a view, are we putting children in a situation where they are pulled between their family (cultural) values and those of the school community.

The Role of Rules

Schools where students are encouraged to use self-management and allowed to make decisions have fewer discipline problems according to some studies. These same studies show that students feel less connected to authoritarian schools in which there are harsh consequences for breaking school rules (McNeely et al. 2002). Nevertheless, schools do need expectations for student behavior. Any group of people has norms of behavior. These norms may be formalized as rules or laws; norms may be informal and understood. It has been often noted that adolescents are concerned about fairness, justice, and participation in a democratic environment. Students in my study were concerned about disruptive students who prevented them from learning: "If there are a lot of troublemakers in the class, you won't be able to learn." Michael Apple and James Beane (1995) have proposed central conditions of democratic schools that include sharing of ideas, group problem solving, concerns for the rights of individuals and minorities, sets of values, and an organizational system that supports a democratic way of life. The challenge for middle schools is to create school communities that embrace such ideals.

As students become responsible participants and experience success in their decision-making abilities, their self-confidence and identity development are enhanced. Students' perceptions of control and their ability to participate in the decision-making process within the school community are related to their motivation to learn and to their attitudes toward school. Some research has shown that discipline problems decreased when students have been involved in school improvement or school restructuring activities (Furtwengler 1991).

Smith (1995) distinguishes between the authoritative and non-authoritative classroom management styles by using adjectives to describe the classroom environment. Authoritative environments are managed, established, organized, maintained, repaired, and disciplined. Non-authoritative environments are described as assisting, nourishing, awakening, and caring. One may conclude that authoritarian, top-down leadership, in the school or in the classroom, is not supportive of a middle school philosophy that promotes a community of learners that includes all participatory groups.

Classroom management and school behavior are major topics in schools and young teachers are concerned with programs or plans that they can take with them into their classrooms. Often these programs are simplistic and generally ineffective in the long run. Across the country, high schools have policemen patrolling the halls and making arrests to keep peace within the school building. It seems that classroom management programs and tactics taken by schools are designed to fix the symptoms of students' defiant behavior rather than to understand the underlying conditions within the learning community that may lead to defiance, vandalism, or even violence.

There is a difference between discipline and punishment, the coercive use of consequences and rewards to control student behavior. The origin of the word discipline is *to teach*, and as educators we are to teach students to make choices about how they behave and to have students participate in the decision-making process. There are many discipline programs available for teachers to use. Assertive Discipline, a classroom management program by Cantor (1979) that was highly promoted in the 1980s, on the surface works and appears to teach; in desperation I used it and even promoted its use by others. I used the phrase, "you choose to behave," but in reality I meant that the students chose to get the rewards. A while ago I attended a state level conference at which a presentation was made about a "wonderful" system for behavior management that was used at a middle school. The students received tickets any time they were *caught being good*. The local businesses donated prizes, and there were other rewards built into the system. At the end of each month, drawings for prizes were held and students who had more "tickets" had more chances to get a prize. The fallacy of the program was evident when the presenter joked that "at the end of the month, you should see the students scrambling to get more tickets. They run around trying to do nice things for people." Reality check! Why are the students trying to be nice? Because they are caring and they respect each other? I hardly think so. The wonderful program taught students that someone should be paid to be nice to others.

According to the 1997 Phi Delta Kappan poll of teachers (Langdon 1997), the problems teachers reported most often involved homework not done, classroom disruptions, talking back or rudeness, and truancy or absenteeism. These results are contrary to the perception that students are violent or criminal that may be suggested when policemen are hired to patrol the halls of schools. If students are not doing their homework and are not coming to school, could the reason be that the homework and school itself are not meeting the needs of the students? When homework consists of copying vocabulary lists or doing thirty rote mathematics problems, students do not see a connection to real life. If students do not see relevance in what they are doing, and feel frustrated that their opinions are not considered, they may avoid the situation by not going to school. I certainly avoid tasks that are unpleasant.

Adolescents are sensitive to criticism and sarcasm. I have observed some teachers who complained that students were rude to them; I thought they were sarcastic and rude to students. I know of a teacher who told an eighth grade student in front of the class, "You have constipation of the brain and diarrhea of the mouth." Yet, this same teacher thought his students should respect him. Students will respect those who show them respect. We must be careful not to generalize. Teachers who responded to the Phi Delta Kappan survey may have had valid reasons for their concerns. Nevertheless, the students may have had different ideas. They were not surveyed.

The moral development of young adolescents, like other areas of development, is in transition. As students observe adults in their environment, whether at home or at school, they learn about what is right and what is wrong. Too often, they see inconsistencies between what adults do and what adults say. I am reminded of a situation in the middle school where I taught. We preached the no smoking message to our students. However, we sat during our breaks in a smoke-filled faculty lounge.

Kohlberg's theory is the basis of most thoughts about adolescent moral development. According to Kohlberg, young children first obey rules because they are afraid of punishment and are primarily concerned about themselves. Later on, children are infatuated with rules. This is clearly seen in elementary schools where young children make up games with special rules or frequently argue about rules of the game. They are intensely interested in fairness. Interest of the effect of rules and fairness on their personal experience is integral in these early ideas about what is right or wrong. As children progress in development, according to Kohlberg, they become interested in pleasing others. According to his theory, those at higher stages of development are more interested in what is ethically important than in blindly following rules (1981). Feminist theorists caution, however, that Kohlberg's theory was based upon studies with males and that girls may respond differently to situations that may make them appear less morally developed than boys. These differences are based on the attitude of care that girls are often culturally prepared to adopt (Gilligan 1982).

Does fair mean equal? When a teacher provides differentiated instruction for students at different levels or with different learning styles is that fair? Not everyone is being treated equally. In a developmentally and culturally responsive school, students will internalize a meaning of fairness that is based upon an understanding of individuality and respect for the needs of others.

Student Perspectives

Sometimes, students send messages that tell teachers about their feelings of belonging but those messages are not received For example, Ira Shor suggests that students who sit on the periphery of the class, who choose to sit in the back of the room, may be acting out a form of resistance to the power hierarchies within the school organization (1992). This mode of expression, when observed by the teacher, can provide some insight into the dynamics of the classroom. Students may express anger or frustration in different ways, and those ways may be based upon gender, cultural, or developmental factors. Some students may express their emotions verbally and others may express them physically. Still others may passively resist the forces that they feel to be oppressive. Educators, who are working to develop a sense of community in their schools and classrooms, address the ways students can express anger not just the symptoms of students' emotions. Such educators address the causes of the anger and defiance (Deffenbacher 1999). By engaging in a dialogue with their students, educators can explore the situations and possible solutions for undesirable reactions in the school.

Initially in my study, student comments about strictness centered on limitations of physical contacts with their friends, hugging, holding hands, etc. Other comments, though, suggested that students were concerned about rules they felt were an inconvenience. Both strictness issues involved control of student actions within the learning environment. Perhaps the control could be related to trust issues; do adults in the school trust students to make decisions about their own behavior?

When I asked students if they would like to have a little more decision-making, they brought up the issue of the school budget. This took me with surprise as I was working with eighth graders and in my typical adult mindset, I thought that such issues would not be interesting to students. When they began to elaborate, they continued to talk about their student council money. The students wanted the student council members to have a bigger say in how their group's money was spent.

"Like [teacher]. He wants to get this rug for the school. It's like thousands of dollars and the student council has enough money for it. But it's just like we don't really need this rug. He just thinks it's the perfect idea. The student council voted all against it. We don't want this rug."

"But they sort of persuaded us into buying it. They said it would make our school look so much better."

"Like the next meeting we had he said, 'Well at the last meeting we voted to get the rug, right?' and we said no and he said 'Well, I'm sure we did' so we just said OK."

"They'll listen to us and say the will do it, but it never happens. Like [participant] said, like we raised money last year for books and desks and they spent it on color printers."

"Yeah, they think we have crappy ideas."

The students seemed to feel that their opinions were not respected because they were "just kids" and they weren't trusted to help make decisions. This example is not unique. I found similar resentment in other schools when students felt they had been used to earn money for the school but had no input into how it was spent, or they were cajoled into spending the money the way the adults in the schools wanted the money to be spent. Young adolescents want to be involved in real-life decision-making. Sarason (1990) agrees that anyone affected by a decision should be involved in the decision-making. Those who have more invested in the decision are more likely to be active, contributing community members. Students in my groups acknowledged that teachers knew things that students did not know. Nevertheless, the students were concerned that their ideas and opinions were not valued. The students were perceptive and angered about their pseudo-participation. They felt betrayed and did not trust the teachers.

Challenge

One of the most difficult tasks in any group is bringing together divergent opinions, views, and values (Strodl 1997). In a pluralistic society, developing a sense of community, of citizenship, requires participation and understanding about the meaning of community. According to Nel Noddings (1992) as teachers become empowered and actively involved in the learning community, students become empowered. As students realize the systems and how they may affect the future of their community, they may become empowered to be learners and change agents. In fact, students often have important insights into what works and what doesn't work. When students have the opportunity to have participatory experiences in their community, they grow to understand the concept of community (Crick 1999).

In my study, students wanted "[Freedom from] people bossing you around. Not like your mother or your father, but bossing." "They won't let you go in the other grade's hall. Like say you have to talk to your brother or sister or something." "I'm already upstairs for my one class...but they won't let me go through the sixth grade hall to my other classes and they are all the way to the other end, down on the bottom, and I have to go all the way back to the end of the place, go down and go all the way to the end." While those who made the rules that the students mention may have had logical reasons for instituting the rules, students did not see the rules in the same light. Because relationships and interactions with peers are paramount in the young adolescents' lives, comments and discussions such as these are not surprising. Students see rules, which may have been designed to improve conditions in the building, as limiting, inconvenient, or unnecessary.

The challenge of citizenship has many societal influences that make the concept of a democratic community difficult. Melinda Fine, in her 1993 study, found that middle school students are able to address controversial issues, but the experience can be volatile. She also proposes that teachers and students must learn to deal with such issues in a constructive manner. Teachers and administrators who believe in a developmentally and culturally responsive middle school take positive action. A school, which is part of larger systems, must also deal with community and political systems through not only the administration but the school board which is elected by the community. If the elected officials trust and respect the educators in the school, the attitude may transfer system-wide. Communication seems to be an integral factor in the development of a sense of community beyond the school walls and in encouraging students to develop ideals of participatory citizenship within their school experience. Effective and productive communication between all stakeholders in the school community may have obstacles. Chapter 7 explores the concept of dialogue and communication in more detail.

CHAPTER 7

Dialogues

Talk is cheap. How many times have we heard that lament? All talk and no action is another quip. We have sayings like "prick up your ears" or "keep one's ears open." Listening is an active process; it takes thinking and effort. We often mistakenly equate listening with hearing. Sometimes, I get irritated when I am talking to people and I sense that they are not really listening, but they are formulating what they are going to say next. A listener pays attention.

As adults we don't always distinguish the difference between talking to students and talking with students. Dialogues are based upon both talking and *listening*. Students, teachers, parents, and the community want to believe their thoughts are seriously considered. I can remember being called to the guidance office in high school to talk about my "future plans." This is the *only* such talk I can remember. The counselor sat opposite me behind her desk and asked where I wanted to go to college. I remember telling her that I was going to the local college. Her reply was, "With SAT scores like yours, you can go anywhere." That did me a lot of good! She didn't ask about what colleges I would like to attend (I had some dreams) or why I chose to go to the local college. She didn't seem to know anything about me or about my dreams, and she didn't take the time to find out. My fifteen minutes were up and she had another student waiting. Dialogues in developmentally and culturally responsive middle schools include talking and listening; dialogues influence action based upon the exchange of ideas.

When I was a middle school teacher, our schedule had a special time called

X-Mod. During this time, teachers and students in their homerooms had no classes. Some might have interpreted such a time as a glorified study hall, but to me it was something different. It was a time I could get to know my students. During the period, we would talk. Sometimes we would play games; sometimes we would do something special like going swimming at the high school pool. Even though I was a math teacher, I always kept an assortment of paperback books that the students could borrow near or in my desk. (I made sure I read them all.) Regularly, students would borrow books from my stash, and I would talk to the students about the books. I found out a good deal about my students by the books they chose and their responses to our discussions. X-Mod also gave us time to talk about what they wanted to discuss. Several years ago, I was at a gathering where I talked to one of my former students who was in his thirties. He asked me if I remembered when we used to talk about his dogs. It's amazing what students remember!

Communication

Through what we say, or don't say, and the way we say it, we inform students of our respect, expectations, and assessments of their culture, possibilities, and achievement. Adolescents have their own vocabulary that seems to be used exclusively to frustrate or shock adults. Words adults may recollect using (sharp, cool, or awesome) make today's teens roll their eyes or giggle. Communication may be strained when we assume that we know what someone means or assume that they know what we mean. When my sons were teenagers, I could name the musicians that they listened to and what movies were considered worth their time. It was they who taught me how to make a webpage and find free clipart on the Internet. It didn't take me long to fall behind in "the latest" when they went off to college and I was left to fend for myself. Now I find myself watching MTV occasionally just to keep in touch. Adolescents like teachers who have a sense of humor. Cartoons or jokes can provide an opening for conversation. What are ways that communication can be encouraged among members of the school community? What is the difference between communication and dialogues? How do dialogues develop in learning communities and how do learning communities benefit from dialogues?

Working together as problem-solvers takes time and effort. Dealing with others in a group also requires an understanding of how groups work. Each person brings his or her own strengths and issues to the discussion. Listening skills are particularly important. However, an understanding of the roles others take in a group is also important. Some persons may be the leaders; others may be the ones who don't say much, but when they do, their comments are well worth considering. Still others may be ones who tend to talk all the time and say nothing: some might just say nothing. A major emphasis in middle school philosophy is the *team approach*. Team building does not come automatically. Just as a goal in developmentally and culturally responsive schools is for students to learn to respect and trust each other and the teachers, a corollary is for teachers to respect and trust each other and their students. When groups have established an atmosphere where dissent and controversy are accepted, or even welcomed, problem solving can flourish.

A developing team or group grows through particular stages. Group members need to get to know each other; sometimes this is difficult as each member is exploring his or her role within the group. Groups also develop their own norms, what is expected of each member and how they will work together. Conflict may arise in a group when members have different goals for themselves and the group as a whole. Group members must feel that they have an equal opportunity to voice their own opinions (Forrest 2002). As team members develop common goals and understanding, they can accomplish more. It seems that group theory, systems theory, and middle school philosophy all agree. Communication and common goals increase productivity.

In their book, *Group Processes in the Classroom* (2001), Richard and Patricia Schmuck emphasize roles that communication plays in classroom interactions and suggest strategies that teachers can use to facilitate positive communication. Many of the strategies, such as cooperative learning and heterogeneous grouping, are ones that have been suggested for developmentally responsive middle school. Donna Eder's book, *School Talk: Gender and Adolescent Culture* (1995), gives an inside view of communication in a middle school. These two books provide an excellent foundation for those who wish to study how adolescents use language to communicate their feelings, expectations, and ideas within groups.

Sticks and stones will break my bones, but words will never harm me. WRONG. Probably one of the most powerful influences on students is what we say. Some words elicit negative or emotional connotations. In addition to the words themselves, voice characteristics, tone inflection may also suggest meanings. Jean Anyon (1995) found this especially troubling in her study of an urban high school in New Jersey. It has already been noted that adolescents are sensitive and may react negatively to sarcasm or criticism by adults. Adolescents also are sensitive to what their peers say. Thurlow (2001) suggests that during adolescence, peer status is important and through language they communicate their impressions of themselves and others. As adolescents attempt to establish their own identity, they often use language to put down others.

Adolescents strive to separate themselves from authority, and language is an effective tool. Slang and other taboo language can be used to show defiance or rebellion (Thurlow 2001). Middle school students will use language just to see if they can shock the teacher and establish their status among their peers. Thurlow reported that boys tend to swear more than girls, but I remember intercepting quite a few notes that girls passed to one another that had rather colorful language.

Thurlow (2001) also found some sex differences in the use of derogatory language among 15-year-olds. Girls were more sensitive in the use of language that referred to homosexuality, and they did not rate such language as seriously as did the boys. Girls are more sensitive to sexist remarks and ethnic minority students were more sensitive to racist remarks. It may be that they are those who have been the target of cruel words. Thurlow suggests that since many homophobic words are aimed at boys, those who have not experienced the hurt are not as sensitive. Strough and Berg (2000) found gender differences in conversation patterns. Boys' conversation was more connected to themselves. Girls' conversations were connected to others and meeting the needs of others. Girls tended to change their conversation patterns when they were in mixed groups while boys did not.

Schmuck and Schmuck (2001) identified four ways that language can communicate sexual bias. Some words are inherently *sex-labeling*. Chairman and housewife are two such words. A colleague and I worked with a group of seventh grade science students. The students were asked to draw a scientist; the majority of students, including most of the girls, drew male scientists. In our society, we assume that scientists are males. Schmuck and Schmuck call this *sex-marking* of words. Another sex bias language pattern is called *omission*. Examples of this bias are found in words such as "mankind;" in such cases the role of "woman" is missing. Finally, sex bias is found when *nonparallel forms* of words are used. A group of women are called "girls" while a group of men in the same setting would not be called "boys." In addition to sexual biases, cultural biases are also presented through language. Instead of saying actor, additional descriptors such as black or Hispanic, are used. In society, it is common to assume that when one mentions an actor, the actor is a white male, so we must put a special note that the actor is not.

The words that are said are important and how those words are interpreted may lead to misunderstanding. Words may have multiple meanings. Think of the word *run*. How many meanings do you know? Move fast; score in baseball; a ruined stocking; a small stream. One's gender or cultural experiences may determine the meaning associated with the word. That is really *bad* may actually mean that something is good in the vernacular of a teenager. Those who speak English may have some trouble understanding what another says. However those whose native languages or dialects are not standard English may even have more difficulty. Anyon gives specific examples of this difficulty in mathematics and science (1995). Idioms or figures of speech may be confusing. We cannot assume that messages sent are the messages received.

Communication may not be vocal; teachers can talk to their students in writing through feedback about the students' work. The way teachers mark papers can give messages to the students. I purposefully do not use red pen or pencil to grade papers. Papers covered with red marks elicit negative responses by the students. (Do they really look at their mistakes and the comments you so thoughtfully included?) One time I found some stickers in my drawer and put them on my eighth graders' papers just as a joke. They snickered when they got their papers back. The next time, I did not put any stickers on the papers. The students howled and complained; I had to go out and buy stickers for the rest of the year. Students like teachers who have a sense of humor, and the stickers were a symbol of my sense of humor.

I know teachers who establish a dialogue with their students through journaling about the students' work. The students and teachers write back and forth about the students' work, and feedback is meaningful. Journaling, when it is used in a meaningful way, can give teachers an insight into what students want to say. However, when journals become a chore, students begin to rebel. One time my son got a poor grade in his middle school English class. During the parent conference, we asked the teacher about the grade. She said the main problem was his journal. He got a D on it because he did not fill a page each day as the assignment said. He is one of those young people whose handwriting needs to be accompanied by a magnifying glass. We have always joked he is a "man of few words" but when he says something, what he says is important. The purpose of the assignment was to fill a page. It didn't matter what the student said. What kind of message does this send to students?

Actions speak louder than words. How many times have we heard that? When we say one thing and do another, we are telling others that we cannot be trusted or that we really didn't mean what we said. Additionally, nonverbal communication such as smiles, gestures, sighs, winks, eye contact, or even posture sends a message. Students may not want to voice their uneasiness or confusion, but by carefully observing their students, teachers can get the message. Teachers can give messages to their students, too, by their actions. Eye contact or just standing at the door to greet students as they enter can say, "I'm happy to see you." I recently talked to someone who lamented that the black students didn't attend the school activity nights or dances. She felt that the reason was probably that the black students did not like the music that was played at the dance, but the teachers didn't like the music that the black students wanted to play. I asked if the teachers had really *listened* to the black students' music; perhaps there could be some music that could be played. I asked her to consider what message the students could be receiving when their music was ignored in favor of the music liked by other groups within the school.

When a student walks into a room, the room itself tells the students something about what the school or teacher is all about; if the room is warm and inviting, students get the message that the teacher and the school care about them. Seating arrangements also support or hinder communication. I like to put my desk off to the side of the room. This arrangement not only gives me more floor space in the room but it removes the barrier between my students and myself. I used the same arrangement in my office as principal and now in my college position. I hope that the arrangement gives messages such as "Come in and let's work together."

Think about times when you have had to sit in chairs that were uncomfortable. You may have thought more about your comfort than what else was going on in the room. Students' desks can also send a message. This is especially important at the middle school level when students are all sizes and shapes. Desks with the tablets attached are uncomfortable when they are the wrong size; big boys in tiny desks just don't work. Adolescents, because of their erratic growth patterns and need to move, need seats that are comfortable. Desks with separate chairs are more versatile. No one likes to talk to the back of someone else's head, so if communication is a goal in the classroom, rows of seats are not the best way to arrange a room. Arranging the desks into tables can allow for group work; a U-shaped arrangement allows for large group instruction and interaction. The teacher can see each student and the students can see each other. Thus, communication, verbal and nonverbal, encourages the development of a supportive learning community.

The Larger School Community

Dialogues are two-way communications in which those involved are anxious to listen and work together. Dialogues within the school community cover a wider range than teachers talking with students. Teachers need to talk with each other, with the community, and with the parents. As a principal, I would often call parents of students who were not the "best" and most of the parents expected the calls to be bad news. They would hesitate and be defensive when I began talking. They would be flabbergasted when I actually gave them good news. One parent shared a story with me after I tried to reach their home but only got the answering machine. I left a message on the machine. She told me that her son saved the taped message and played it every time they got company. My few minutes had more effect than I could have imagined. My good news was reinforced many times over.

Middle school literature emphasizes the importance of working with and within the community. A key point in the Carnegie Council's *Great Transitions: Preparing Adolescents for a New Century* (1998) is the importance of involvement of parents in the school community. At a minimum, schools expect parents to come to annual back to school nights or parent-teacher conferences. Typically, it is at the middle school level when parent attendance at parent-teacher conferences declines, although parent attendance at activities such as sporting events may increase. Sometimes, although schools *say* they want more parent involvement, they are uncomfortable with actual involvement and don't want parents to *meddle*. In reality, parents can be assets to the school when lines of communication have been established. Parents can show their involvement with their children's education without coming to the school. Housebound parents can run a phone tree or prepare materials. The possibilities are endless.

The physical arrangement in conferences is often the condition that alienates parents. Teachers sit behind their desks; parents sit to the side or in the front in uncomfortable student-sized chairs. The teacher is in the position of power—behind the desk—the parent is in the position of the student. Rather than creating the perception that parents and teachers are partners in a child's education, parents get the message that they are less important. Perhaps this feeds into the parents' uncomfortable perception that teachers are the "experts" who look down upon the knowledge that parents can bring to the conference.

As I work with pre-service teachers, I encounter "teacher beliefs" that I heard from experienced teachers frequently: The parents who don't come to conferences aren't interested in their children; you never see the parents you want to see; only the parents of *good* students come to conferences; parents and parent groups want to tell teachers how to teach. It is time to dispel some of these myths.

School conferences may be scheduled at times when parents are just not able to come to school. Employers may not be willing to give parents personal time to visit schools; parents may not be able to afford the lost wages for the time they spend at the schools; transportation across town may be difficult; parents may have physical or health issues that prevent them from coming; or parents may not be able to speak English and be worried that they would embarrass their children. Childcare could be a problem. Such reasons are not excuses but may be valid concerns that we as educators overlook. In supportive middle schools, educators acknowledge obstacles, become problem-solvers, and work within the community to make themselves accessible to parents. Non-traditional times can be scheduled to work around parents' schedules. Instead of telling parents when they are to come for a conference, responsive teachers ask parents when they can come or where they could meet.

Even before a conference, the challenge for middle level educators is to engage parents in conferencing. Many parents, who may not have had positive experiences themselves in school, do not want to come to school. If parents do not want to come to school, teachers can go to the parents. Teachers can meet with parents, formally or informally, in parents' comfort zones—community centers, churches, or community events. Teachers can meet parents and learn about the community at street fairs, craft fairs, firemen's carnivals, ethnic festivals, or discount stores. When I started my first teaching job, I knew no one in the community. I learned that the parent group was having a strawberry festival the week before school started so I wandered through the festival. I stopped to talk to one parent as she sold tickets. This woman was a great supporter of students and the school; she and I remained friends until her recent death. Teachers who seek to understand their students' communities enter into the community.

What's wrong with the parents of *good kids* coming to conferences? My husband and I tried to attend every conference for our children. If both of us couldn't go, at least one of us did. One time when our son, Matthew, was in high school, I had to be out of town, and my husband had other commitments, so we decided not to attend. Big mistake! My son was disappointed. Whether they want to admit it or not, all students want to believe that their parents care. Too many times parent conference is equated with *problem* rather than *conversation.* Conferences are times to learn about all students.

Students are usually excluded from the mysterious parent-teacher conference, yet students are the focus. Students worry about what the teacher is saying or how the parent will interpret what the teacher says. Many developmentally and culturally responsive middle schools include students in the conferences. Students believe that their ideas and opinions are important and they can explain their learning to their parents. This allows parents who may have negative memories of school, a safety valve. The parent will not need to talk only with the teacher; the parent will talk with the student. Students can share their successes with their parents and can be part of problem-solving decisions. Parent-student-teacher conferences may also give non-English speaking parents access to the school in a non-threatening way because students can act as translators.

Interactions with parents should not be limited to discussion of students' academic progress. These opportunities for dialogue can be used to develop relationships, to learn about parents' concerns or dreams about their children, and to allow parents to be partners. As parents begin to feel more valued in their children's education, they may be more willing to come to the school and take an active role in the school community. In a culturally diverse school, parents can share information about their heritages to increase understanding and the effectiveness of learning activities.

Although the ideal may be to have face-to-face conferences, phone conferences may be an alternative. The conversations can be arranged for times that are convenient for both parents and teachers. Some teachers use technology to communicate with parents. The teachers create websites that give important information to parents and links to resources. Also, some teachers suggest that parents contact them by email and also contact the parents by email. Caution must be taken, however, for some students and parents may not have access to the technology.

Community and business involvement can be a plus for a middle school that strives to meet the needs of all students. Opportunities for students to work with service agencies where students can interact with community members of different ages and needs can allow students to explore their own interests and identities. Activities that allow students to make real-life connections with what they are learning in classes make learning meaningful. However, when businesses focus on influencing school curriculum and organization to meet the needs of the businesses, caution must be taken. When businesses are using their economic power to influence school curriculum and organization in order to produce workers for their businesses rather than students who are critical thinkers and are prepared for the global society, educators, students, and parents must critically analyze the involvement. Communication among educators and community members is essential to develop clear understandings about the purposes, expectations, and benefits of community-based activities.

Schools have been under criticism; teacher and school accountability are political issues. As educators we are sometimes afraid of too much community or parent involvement because we are afraid of being scrutinized or having our professionalism questioned. It is at such times that we, as professionals, must make even more effort to communicate, to have dialogues, with community members. When parents and the community feel part of the school, they are less likely to criticize or complain. They get opportunities to see the real life between the *hallowed walls*. It is very common to find editorials and columns in local newspapers that purport to report conditions within schools or to evaluate education. Quite often, persons who have little knowledge of what actually happens in a classroom write these articles. Opinions are formed without extensive research or study. Educators seem to believe that because they are teachers, they are not permitted to voice their opinions publicly; this is not the case. Public opinion and politics are molding classroom practices. Educators who do not use their voices to influence their profession cannot complain.

Dialogues with Colleagues

When I was a middle school teacher, the teachers had a bowling league. We looked forward to going bowling once a week to have time together as adults. Too often as teachers, we are isolated from one another and do not have time or the inclination to talk to each other either in or out of school. Professional conversations are often limited to faculty room talk or team meetings where specific tasks must be accomplished in limited times. Opportunities for teachers to meet together for professional growth are scheduled with curriculum meetings, speakers, or workshops. Administrators, who recognize the importance of collaboration and teacher dialogue, find time to schedule regular opportunities for teachers to work together. The first time I had the opportunity to develop a schedule as a principal, I struggled to find time for grade level meetings and assigned teachers to weekly meetings. One of the teachers came to me and said the time allotted for meetings was foolish, and no one was going to tell him he had to go to a meeting and waste one period a week. Later, this teacher was one of the greatest supporters of the team concept. When teachers have the opportunity to work together productively, and see what can be accomplished, teachers grow professionally.

As a teacher, I was fortunate to have a principal who encouraged collaboration between teachers to improve instruction. He asked for volunteers and then arranged for two-person teams of teachers to work together in a peer-coaching activity. Together, we studied effective practices and observational skills. We learned to trust each other. We each visited our partner's classroom and gave feedback based on individual classroom goals. We learned from each other. This supportive principal provided time for us to work together and the financial support for us to attend workshops. Our principal communicated his respect and trust for teachers by his support and actions. His desire to support teachers in their professional growth ultimately led to my earning principal certification, and I tried to model my principalship after many of his practices that encouraged teachers to work and learn together.

Not long ago, I was invited to present a workshop to a group of teachers. I could tell by their body language and conversation when they entered the room that they resented being assigned to the workshop. In one of those on-the-spot decisions, I varied from my plan and tried to meet their needs. We "covered the topic," but I did not take the role of the expert. I gave them time to talk. I told them that I was facing a room of experts and as peers we would discuss the information and they could share their concerns and ideas. I used my material, but they gave each other support as we had a professional discussion. They told me they enjoyed the workshop, and some even asked me to send them some additional information; I gained good ideas I could take back to my college classroom.

As professionals, middle level educators can work together to learn more about their school, community, and students. Recently, I learned of a school district that was planning to change from the junior high concept to the middle school concept. For about two years before the planned time for change, teachers and administrators studied together, attended conferences together, and created a vision for their school. As colleagues working toward a shared vision, they made decisions that would affect the lives of the students they would teach. Administrative support to provide the time for such study was a plus. I also learned of a school in which regularly a group of teachers met for breakfast to discuss a book they had all read. They figured they all had to eat anyway, and it didn't take too much effort to come to school a little early.

I teach a curriculum course that is required of all secondary teacher certification candidates on our campus. As part of the course, students are learning to use technology to make their lives as teachers easier and use a program for on-line learning as an enhancement to class activities. Students have on-going discussions about their assignments, projects, and even ethical and social issues. They carry on thoughtful and provocative discussions that I hesitate to enter. They have found that these on-line discussions can be held at any time of the day from anywhere on the Internet. Students who may not be comfortable entering into a live conversation feel at ease. One of my students said she likes to take ideas and let them roll around in her mind for a while before she responds, and live conversations sometimes leave her behind. The electronic conversation makes her feel part of the class. These students are learning to enter into professional conversations with their colleagues for the first time. Many teachers I know belong to on-line chat groups or forums where they share ideas; the Internet makes professional resources available no matter where one lives; and teachers can access their professional organizations with a click of a button.

Creative educators find time to interact with their colleagues whether electronically or in person. Administrators who wish to develop a collaborative community provide support for those who wish to work together and incentives for those who may be hesitant. No matter how they do it, teachers who develop relationships can become vital influences on the health of the school community. As they work together to be problem solvers, they become models for their students. As students see their teachers working together and enjoying the camaraderie that develops, the adolescents can see the importance of dialogue.

Talking with Students

Although it is extremely important to work with our colleagues, parents, and community members, the adolescents within our schools are the primary emphasis. As educators, our credentials testify to our level of achievement within the educational system. We have made the grades, passed the tests, and communicated our "worthiness" in order to get our jobs. Some of us have negotiated this path with relative ease. Nevertheless, memories fade and become distorted. If we look among us, we will find little diversity and a few gray hairs. We, by age, background, and position are divorced from the adolescent experience in school. We cannot turn back the clocks, nor may we wish to do so. We can learn about adolescent experiences, albeit vicariously, through the voices of our students.

In 1998, I spent time with groups of eighth graders to get a glimpse of their perceptions of their middle school learning environment. Not surprisingly, I found that the students had different perceptions of their school life than did the teachers. First, I surveyed teachers and students using the same instrument and found areas on the survey that suggested different perceptions. I found great discrepancies related to teachers talking to students. Students wanted teachers to talk to them and felt that the teachers were not while the teachers thought they were. One student remarked about a teacher, "He don't talk to us about nothing" to which another replied, "He's sort of old or something." The conversation continued when another student commented that teachers "just talk to us about stuff that doesn't interest us." Such comments imply that a cultural or generational chasm exists that may cause differences in perceptions. Although teachers in fact *may* talk to their students, students often do not receive the messages.

Validating the voices of students is of primary importance in conversations to effect change; listening to students and respecting their opinions are essential. Conversation must move beyond sharing information and defending positions to a creative level of interaction. Jenlink and Carr (1995) suggest that for change to occur conversations must involve dialogue during which assumptions are examined without judgment. Through examining individual assumptions and opinions without confrontation or evaluation while honoring diversity, a group can develop meaning for the school community.

During the rash of school shootings in the late 1990s, it became clear that in most cases, students in the school knew information that may have prevented tragedies, but they did not tell the adults in the school. Why? A key element supporting dialogues is relationships built upon trust. In many cases, students do not feel comfortable talking to the adults in their schools. In my study, students were concerned about confidentiality: "If I tell the counselor, she will just tell my mother." In a developmentally responsive middle school, students and teachers are clear about the boundaries for confidentiality. Students must be aware of what kind of information can be shared and what teachers are legally bound to divulge. Other than those specifics, students should be comfortable that their concerns will not be fodder for faculty room gossip. One time I had a very angry parent call me. Her sister was at a beauty salon and overheard a conversation between a teacher and her beautician. The teacher did not realize the relationship between the other patron and the student. The confidential information that was being shared quickly was told to the student's mother. I to do a great deal of problem solving to defuse the situation. A careless act gave messages to students, parents, and the community that confidentiality is not part of the school environment.

Sometimes, the reason students don't perceive that teachers talk to them as much as students might wish could be the topics of conversations. Talking with students, in students' eyes, is a characteristic of teachers who care and take personal interest in their students. When students in my study did perceive that the teachers talked to them, the subjects dealt with not only their schoolwork but their lives: "He'll take the time to talk to me about my school work…then he'll ask me about what I did on the weekend…and what I like and stuff." One teacher talks to me about what's going on. Like she knows my family and stuff…stuff that is going on in the family and things." "Well, like my computer teacher… Everyday when I am walking down the hall, he'll stop me and say if I have any problems in school, come to him." "He'd always be friendly to you…walk up to you…try to help you no matter what…He'd' sit there and answer you back and say stuff like that's a good job and stuff like that…and he brought in his fish. It was a huge fish."

Students can tell what works and what doesn't work. "She is so boring. All she does is write on the board and say the same things over and over." "And her voice never changes. Blah, blah, blah." I have heard teachers complain that their job is to educate not to entertain students. How does one teach if students are not listening? Undoubtedly there are times when the best strategy for an objective is for the teacher to talk. Lectures may be an effective strategy when used appropriately. Teachers can change from teacher-centered to student-centered lessons. An understanding of the development of the young adolescent helps teachers adapt the lesson to meet the students' needs: identifying the purpose of the lesson, breaking the lesson into smaller parts, including questions from the students, and encouraging students to interact with the material can change a "boring," teacher-centered lecture into one students see as effective.

To change the pattern of teacher-talk, adults must be open to student culture and the ways students express their ideas and needs. Apple and Beane (1995) suggest that educators have their responsibility to help students listen to the opinions of others and develop the ability to voice their own opinions. This may require teachers to change the way classrooms are structured or curriculum is organized. Cooperative learning has often been suggested as a strategy.

However, because adolescents are intrigued by real-life situations, they may not relate to cooperative learning activities that seem contrived. In problem-based learning projects during which students address real-life problems, teachers assume a different role. Teachers design or organize the project and facilitate the learning experience and then become encouragers and resource persons. Teachers interject thought provoking questions to promote higher-order thinking. Middle school students have investigated pollution in local streams or local zoning ordinances to solve problems. They have gone beyond what would be expected of students their age. The community becomes the classroom.

Student beliefs about the impact of school practices influence their perceptions, motivations, and experiences. Students often interpret the learning environment to include barriers to their own success, especially when their beliefs are in contrast with the dominant ideology of the school. One student reported, "I wanted to play football in 6th and he [the teacher] told the boys I shouldn't be able to play...He didn't like me because I was a girl." Students recognize inequalities. In fact, during my study boys were the first to suggest that girls were treated differently. Discussions about social class, gender, religion, race, or ethnicity may be uncomfortable in a school setting for adults. Political and economic forces that influence school decision-making may lead to ignoring issues or addressing them in superficial manners. Nevertheless, in an atmosphere of trust, students willingly share their beliefs about the impact of issues such as gender or social class upon practices within the school.

It is the intersection of multiple identities that influences each individual — identities influenced by gender, race, social class, or ethnicity. In order to understand the uniqueness of each individual, educators must listen to the "stories" their students tell about their own lived experiences. O'Connor identified several "conarratives" which demonstrate a "substantive variation" in how young people make sense of their opportunities and how this variation results from their multiple identities and personal experiences related to variables such as social class, gender, and race (1999, 142–153).

According to Patricia Hinchey, "School culture, like all others, is permeated with beliefs and assumptions often mistaken for fact" (1998, 3). One of the most pervasive beliefs is that children should be seen but not heard. As educators, we often make choices about what happens in our classrooms from our own perspectives without accessing the perspectives of the students (1998). In order to make choices that meet the needs of our students, we must listen to the varied perspectives brought to classrooms.

Students suggest that teachers may not understand issues related to students' lives. Teachers "...just talk to us about stuff that doesn't interest us," according to students in my study. Henry Giroux states that youth "often find themselves being educated and regulated within institutions that have little relevance for their lives" (1996, 13). Curriculum and other trappings of schooling often support a dominant culture that to some students is alienating. Instead of being places where students can explore diversity and multiple sources of knowledge, schools urge conformity. Often, Giroux continues, schools actually marginalize or exoticize youth culture and diversity in their attempts to be politically correct.

Challenge

Many researchers suggest that students are not often asked about their perceptions of their learning environments (Ayers 1990; Fraser 1994; Lincoln 1995). Yet students' experiences, and their perceptions of those experiences, determine their relationships and success within school programs. The Carnegie Council recommends that a school be a "community of learners" (1989, 37) and the National Middle School Association (NMSA) suggests that a school climate should promote "a sense of community" and encourage learning by involving all stakeholders in shared decision-making (1995, 18). Students and teachers should engage in dialogue to create opportunities for learning; this dialogue must be one in which people are willing to listen to each other's positions and explore shared meanings (Banathy 1996). When participants are able to understand circumstances and conditions in personal contexts as well as in light of the perspectives of others, real learning occurs (Sergiovanni 1996).

Yvonna Lincoln (1995) suggests that educators are often reluctant to seek input from students. Even so, it is not uncommon for voices of young people to be heard in other venues. Young adolescents are often asked about their preferences in child custody cases. When making marketing decisions, businesses certainly listen to the preferences of youth. Why is it then that educators are hesitant to listen to students? Are we afraid that the students will only be concerned about chewing gum or shirking work? I suggest otherwise as do Michael Apple and James Beane (1995). Ira Shor (1996) and many others believe students can provide valuable information about what works and what does not work in schools. Students can provide insights into their perceptions of the learning community. Are teachers, who may feel they have limited power, afraid to share power with their students? Ira Shor suggests this may be the case. As educators we must challenge our own values, beliefs, and assumptions about the role students play in forming the learning environment.

Strategies for building community and communication in school are no secret. Literature about effective schools for adolescents suggests there are many ways to provide opportunities for teachers and students to interact in both formal and informal situations. Organizations such as the Carnegie Council on Adolescent Development (1989), the National Middle School Association (1995), and the National Association of Secondary School Principals (1993) and authors such as James Beane (1993) and Ted Sizer (1992) provide practical means to develop curriculum to support a learning community. Beyond consensus building and developing shared views, conversations must move to create; to move beyond what is to what could be. "Design" conversations encourage participants to dream and look to the future (Banathy 1996; Jenlink and Carr 1996).

Relationships based on respect and care demand reciprocity between teachers and students (Beane 1993; Noddings 1992). An atmosphere of trust and respect facilitates open discourse within which students and teachers share ideals and beliefs, though without understanding individual ideologies, this knowledge does not become emancipatory (Taylor, Dawson, and Fraser 1995).

The challenge then for educators is to examine existing conditions and determine barriers in the learning environment that may hinder communication and dialogue. However, a critical educator looks beyond what exists and investigates power systems, biases, and assumptions that influence the environment. The challenge is to take action. This may require flexibility and change. Flexibility and change are the focus of Chapter 8.

CHAPTER 8

Flexibility and Change

In the summer of 2002, I attended a national conference for teacher educators in Williamsburg, Virginia. The opening session was held in the former Bruton Heights High School. I did not know much about the building. As I walked in, I saw a showcase of memorabilia and observed several people looking at the display. I noticed one distinguished looking black woman pointing out pictures of people she knew—her cousin and her aunt. It finally dawned on me that this school was formerly a black high school.

As the program began, I sat in the auditorium and realized that the person I had observed in the lobby was the president of the national organization, the Association of Teacher Educators. She shared with us that she had attended Bruton Heights School when it was segregated. (Williamsburg's schools did not become integrated until 1966, although the landmark Supreme Court Case, *Brown v. Board of Education*, was decided in 1954.) I reflected on my own high school days; I graduated from high school the same year the Bruton Heights School became integrated. I wondered how she must have felt as she returned to the school where she had experienced segregation; there she was not able to attend schools with white students and now she was the president of a national organization for teacher educators. I tried to understand how I might have felt if I were in such a situation but realized that I couldn't really feel the same as she must have felt. My "whiteness" did not force me to go to a "separate but equal (?)" school.

At the same conference, I had the opportunity to meet an energetic woman who was retired from the university I had attended as an undergraduate. We had a frank discussion about her experiences and how that university and town have changed since I left. In the 1960s it was an "understanding" that black professors could not buy homes near the university; now she and her husband live in an integrated development in the same community. She tells me the environment has changed; the community pool is integrated; the campus is much more diversified. Clearly, growing up in my hometown now is different from my experiences. Nevertheless, she still experiences occasional discrimination and insults.

Times change. Our world is constantly changing. I hear and read about education for the twenty-first century. What exactly does this mean? It seems that every time I thumb through an article about change in education, I find reference to "thinking out of the box." However, the story of Pandora lurks in the recesses of our minds warning us not to be too curious, not to open that box. When Pandora opened her mythical box, all kinds of vices and diseases were unleashed and only hope remained inside.

Sometimes it's easier to rely on others to solve our problems so we don't have to take the responsibility for the outcomes. We feel secure if we only tinker with the system. The future of schools and society is the responsibility of all of us. According to the myth of Pandora, Zeus ordered Hephaestus to create an evil being whom all men would desire. Pandora was that beautiful and cunning creature. She opened the box and evil escaped. Does this myth warn us to be wary of change? Are we afraid of what "evils" may emerge if we open the box? We sometimes forget that Pandora's box also contained hope.

Clearly, the purpose of schooling determines the direction for our actions. It seems that members of society have not come to consensus about what that purpose may be. Contrasting purposes seem to both preserve society and change society. Can we preserve our values and ideals *and* change to meet the needs of a future society? Whose values and ideals should be preserved? Should our values and ideals be changed? No doubt, society will change. Schools can either change or be left behind. I am the product of the "Sputnik Era." As an adolescent, I experienced accelerated science programs and "new math." I believe I am an educated person—but would my twentieth-century education meet the needs of today's adolescents? What is the aim of education for the twenty-first century?

I dragged out an old copy of John Dewey's *Democracy and Education* published in 1916 and began to think of what he would have to say to us today.

He says we must assess existing conditions and look to the future. What are the possibilities for the future? What are the obstacles? What are the different paths we could take? Dewey says we need to have a plan but we should be flexible. We should look at the possible consequences for the paths we take and take responsibility for what we do.

I took stock of existing conditions. Education is supposed to be a priority if one listens to political campaigns that talk of high standards, accountability, vouchers, and equal opportunities. Some suggest that students in the United States are not meeting international standards and are being surpassed by students in Third World countries. If this is true, harbingers of doom suggest that something must be wrong with the educational system in our country. Thus, the rationale is that politicians must "fix" the problem.

The Issues

Perhaps a fundamental issue in the current debate is the difference between education and schooling. These two terms are often confused. Education is a personal process—gaining knowledge and understanding; learning to solve problems, learning to communicate ideas, and being able to grow. Teachers can facilitate education but cannot force one to be "educated." Schooling is how we attempt to accomplish education, but education is not necessarily accomplished through schooling in classrooms in school buildings. Do current reform initiatives address education or schooling? Are we focused on the accouterments or the essence of learning?

If education is a personal process that can be "facilitated," what knowledge are we going to facilitate? First, we must look at what knowledge is made accessible to our students. High national standards are supposed to be the aim. Who is setting those standards? Will the standards meet future needs? Instead of discussing the assessment of what our students know and are able to do, we should address what our students *will need* to know and be able to do. How will we be able to predict those needs unless we open the box to explore?

Do our standards espouse one philosophy or worldview? Will the basics of today be the basics in the new century? Some "back to basics" proponents do not want our standards to encourage children to use critical thinking because then the children may challenge current values. Do any of our current values need to be challenged? Are we going to perpetuate the myth that too much curiosity will thwart the intelligent mind? In our effort to offend no one, have we made our standards anachronistic? Who is going to make decisions about what knowledge is valued? Will we sit idly and allow politicians, businesses, and special interest groups to make the decision?

If we assume that the standards we set for our students are valid, how are we going to know that students meet our standards? Some politicians say we need accountability, and testing students and teachers provides accountability. Do test scores tell the whole story? What is on these tests? Who makes the tests? Who takes the tests? How do these tests predict success in the future? Are there alternate ways of determining the success of our schooling?

Over the last twenty or so years, some aspects of schooling have changed. Howard Gardner (1991) proposed his theory of multiple intelligences. The terms "authentic assessment" and "performance assessment" have entered our vocabulary. The mantra of high expectations for all is heard. Qualitative research and teacher action research are gaining respectability. Teachers are told that they are facilitators of learning. Nevertheless, an emphasis on standardized testing with quantifiable results is resurging. The 2001 No Child Left Behind Act (US Department of Education 2002) requires research-based, statistical evidence that schools and children are succeeding.

The materials and methods we use for schooling certainly have changed; I no longer use "purple dittos." Our reliance on textbooks is waning; technology is emerging as a potential force in schooling. The role of teachers will change as teachers guide their students through the multitudes of innovations. Information is at our fingertips. Teachers will need to help their students search for, evaluate, and use this new information. Creativity may help us exceed our expectations.

Just as our society and schools are becoming diverse and experiencing change, diversity and change are indigenous within the adolescent experience. Since growth within an individual student may be erratic and students have their own cultural heritages, the combination of many individuals within the classroom requires teachers to adapt programs, strategies, and materials to address the diversity; thus, there is need for flexibility.

If the learning environment is to be flexible, members of school communities who are concerned with their respective school's effectiveness may need to investigate their roles in the learning environment. Feminist pedagogy, multicultural pedagogy, community theory, systems theory, constructivist theory, and critical theory challenge the taken-for-granted interpretations of schooling and challenge educators to look at how both teachers and students construct the reality of school.

In the Schools and Classrooms

The task for middle level educators, who are faced with young adolescents with diverse backgrounds and needs, is to acknowledge the challenges, find ways to address the challenges, and to incorporate strategies and organizational patterns within a learning environment that supports all students. According to Fraser (1990), the learning environment must be flexible to meet the needs of students through a differentiation of teaching strategies based upon the abilities, interests, learning styles, and rates of learning of the students. This is not quite complete; we must also adapt our curriculum, teaching strategies, materials, and assessment based upon the cultural, gender, and socio-economic differences of our students.

A learning community that supports risk-taking and exploration provides opportunities for flexibility. Administrators are instructional leaders who establish a safe environment that provides time and support for discussion, professional development, and implementation of new ideas. Teachers are willing to take risks and believe they are supported in their attempts to create an environment that will support the varying needs of their students; needs that change day-to-day and often minute-to-minute. A learning environment that is flexible provides opportunities for success in multiple ways; it changes based on democratic decision-making; it supports relationships in which participants trust and respect each other. The challenge of flexibility may indeed be the keystone of a learning environment that meets the needs of young adolescents.

Differentiation in a supportive learning environment requires a commitment to flexibility. Flexibility is necessary to support the needs of young adolescents. Developmental theories seem to agree that there is no "typical" young adolescent. Each student is unique within a wide range of expected characteristics, and the challenge for a school to provide for the individual while dealing with groups of students is formidable, but not unattainable.

Middle school philosophy has long proposed flexible organizational structures, but often these suggestions are considered impractical or difficult to implement. Now, more than ever, these suggestions are appropriate. The Carnegie Council (1989) recommended small groups of students and teachers who work together as teams. In a school devoted to meeting the needs of diverse students, these teams include students from all groups within the school community. Students and teachers have the opportunity to work with those who are different; to share goals and accomplishments; to share concerns; to learn about each other; and learn to care about each other.

Relationships between teachers and students are valued. In some responsive schools, teachers may be assigned to teams of students for more than one year. This practice has been promoted in primary schools as "looping" so teachers can follow the development of the young children. Such practice is also appropriate for young adolescents. Other schools provide times where teachers and students can interact informally to build relationships based upon respect and trust.

Tracking of students, often a mechanism for legitimizing inequality, is eliminated in a school devoted to meeting the needs of diverse students. Heterogeneous grouping, using groups within groups, is the typical strategy. Grouping would be done for specific purposes; new groups would regularly be formed. Rather than "minority" students and students from lower socio-economic groups being in lower-tracked classes where research suggests teachers tend to have lowered expectations, students with all talents and abilities work together and all students are expected to achieve.

In a school devoted to meeting the needs of all students, blocks of time are flexible. Block scheduling and extended periods are options but rather than having classes fit the block, the blocks fit the needs of the classes. Time is provided for students and teachers to interact informally, both during the school day and after school hours. In some schools, teachers regularly eat lunch with students or attend dances and sporting events whether it is a duty or not (Noddings 1992). Other schools have instituted student advisory programs. Still others have activity programs during which students and teachers explore common interests (George and Alexander 1993). Schools are connected to the community through communication and interaction.

Curriculum cannot be static; it must change as the needs of the students change. Each year, each group and each individual brings unique issues to the school experience; students also bring their needs and concerns that tend to be dynamic. The school program, in order to address these concerns, must be prepared to adapt, to be flexible and connect learning to the lives of the students.

In middle school philosophy, key curriculum considerations include making the curriculum relevant to students' lives and building upon students' interests. Likewise, these suggestions are applicable to schools that strive to meet the needs of diverse students. Rather than simply adding Asian, Black, or Native American "decorations" to literature courses, a culturally relevant curriculum builds on the life experiences of students; the curriculum gives validity and honor to their culture and experience. Content is approached critically; students learn to examine content for bias and power systems.

Multicultural literature, art, music, and philosophy can easily be incorporated into thematic approaches to learning that are proposed by middle school philosophy. Such curriculum provides opportunities for work and activities to be organized around student interests. As teachers and students investigate ideas through different disciplines, students with different interests, backgrounds, and needs can have opportunities to see connections among not only the subject matter but among people and cultures.

The inclusion of literature for students who may be biracial has often been lacking in curricula. It is important that, in our quest to be "multicultural," our curriculum doesn't place racial and ethnic groups into divisive categories. Often, such a categorical approach places children in a no man's land, a place where they do not fit. Rather than holding up isolated "role-models" for "minority" students, curricula should reflect multicultural people in a variety of real-life situations. Culturally responsive schools do not limit "multicultural" discussions to Black History Month, Women's History Month, or Cinco de Mayo. Instead, cultural heritages are explored throughout the curriculum (Wardle 1992).

A culturally responsive curriculum moves beyond stereotypes and generalizations. Hispanic students are not all from Mexico or Puerto Rico; Asian students are not all from China or Japan. Students who do not speak English may already be bilingual or even multilingual. An effective curriculum focuses on concepts and understandings set within the socio-cultural environment. For example, rather than arguing about theoretical (and often political) issues related to the form of bilingual education adopted by a school, schools should be focusing on finding what works with students in particular environments. What works in one school may not work in another. The goal of curricula should be providing opportunities for students to excel (McLaughlin and McLeod 2002).

Consistent with middle school literature, findings in my 1998 research suggest that students want choices about what they study, but at the same time are hesitant to suggest what they want to study or investigate. Talking with students, listening to students, learning about their out-of-school activities and communities, and being involved with the students' activities give teachers glimpses of what students may wish to discuss but are hesitant to suggest. As students and teachers become more comfortable with each other, students may feel more willing to make suggestions.

In a middle school for a diverse society, the curriculum provides opportunities for students to put into action their understandings of social equality. Instead of just saving the manatees or the air from pollution (although these are important) a culturally relevant curriculum enables students to deal with issues of conflict, relationships, and diversity at a developmentally appropriate level.

Flexibility of materials can range from kinds of tools used by the teachers to present concepts to the language used by the teachers and students. Methodologies that support the individual needs of the students often include opportunities for variations in time allotted for the completion of activities. Tensions may result from the infusion of differentiated time and materials into the school curriculum. Although literature about middle level education acknowledges diversity in the intellectual development of young adolescents, a fear exists that flexibility or differentiation of methods and materials will lower standards. Instead of focusing on the verbal and quantitative intelligences that have traditionally been the basis of measuring success, alternate approaches such as those of Howard Gardner's multiple intelligence theory (1991) prove to be viable ways for students to show a high level of achievement. As students and teachers become more comfortable with alternate approaches to instruction and assessment, tensions may lessen.

Student perceptions about the appropriateness of differentiated materials, strategies, or time may be colored by students' ideas of fairness or equality. If students believe that differentiated approaches to meet individual needs are not just, then they may react negatively. Teachers and students in a supportive learning community who have had the opportunity to learn to understand and evaluate the use of differentiate materials and strategies. Misunderstandings may be mediated by the learning environment which supports a community of learners, a community that is based upon relationships; a community where people know and care about one another (Apple and Beane 1995); Battistich et al. 1995; Sergiovanni 1996). Yvonna Lincoln suggests that when some participants are silenced and marginalized, conflict, contradictions, and lack of consensus exists (1989). When students are able to understand things in their own personal context as well as consider the knowledge in light of the perspectives of others, real learning occurs (Sergiovanni 1996).

In the era of political emphasis on student achievement and teacher accountability, assessment of student progress has turned toward an emphasis on standardized tests. These tests are being used to measure the "effectiveness" of schools and curriculum; the definition of effectiveness leaves much to be desired. A developmentally and culturally appropriate middle level school provides students with multiple opportunities for demonstrating their knowledge and experiencing success.

Schools and the students in them have become items in political platforms. I recently learned of a school district where the teachers were told not to "waste their time" teaching anything that wasn't tested on the state examinations. Student scores on the examinations were used to determine amounts of money local schools received from the state. Student learning was not the focus; students were instruments for funding. Teachers are asked to post the standards for each lesson on the board; students recite the standard they are learning. The implication of such messages is that if learning cannot be crystallized into a "standard" that is posted on a board, the learning is not valuable. Additionally, teachers who do not specifically identify a standard are "dumbing down" or watering down a curriculum. The affective dimension of school, the development of positive relationships and understanding, cannot be measured quantitatively; therefore, the message is "don't waste your time." The message implies that schools that address cultural understanding and interpersonal relationships do not have high standards.

School financing throughout the United States has historically been discriminatory. Jonathan Kozol brought this to the attention of the public in his seminal book, *Savage Inequalities*, in 1991 yet not much has changed. Still many urban and poor rural schools lack the funding for adequate materials, reasonable class sizes, and well-trained teachers. Instead, school districts are turning to teachers with "emergency" or "alternative" certifications and to privatization of schools. Schools and the students in them have become an item in political platforms. Some suggest that businesses, whose bottom line is money, can provide better education for students. The effectiveness of the businesses is measured by improvement of standardized test scores. Rather than investigating and dealing with the socio-economic issues that may be impacting upon student achievement, businesses and politicians look for a quick fix.

Some school reformers propose that perhaps it is our public school system that is at fault, and providing students and parents with a choice would be the solution. School choice by use of vouchers is a myth. Few of the students who cannot afford to attend private schools now will be able to afford private schools with a voucher that only covers a portion of the bill. Additionally, research shows that minority students who can afford to pay costs tend to choose white schools and white students who can afford the costs tend to choose white schools. Thus, the schools students leave behind are populated with a higher percentage of low income, minority students (Saporito and Lareau 1999). The old adage, the rich get richer and the poor get poorer applies.

Open enrollment programs by which students can choose any public school within a district don't fare much better. Those who cannot afford the transportation across town or whose parents can't take them to school don't transfer. Parents and students from affluent neighborhoods don't choose to go to schools that are run-down or "in the bad part" of town.

Change within the existing system may be a solution. However, the system of the future may look entirely different. In the new century, buildings as we see them now may be obsolete; materials will be different; and even curricula will be different. Technology supposedly will be the mechanism for change. Again, gender, ethnic, and socio-economic forces will mediate the changes. Traditionally, fewer girls take computer courses. Data show that computer ownership and Internet access is related to family income, family structure, race, and place of residence. In some cities, free access to the Internet is available, but rural, poor students have less access than most   (US Department of Commerce 2001).

In addition to a digital divide, schools and classrooms may be faced with a dogmatic divide. Perhaps this divide is more injurious than the technical, digital divide. When positivistic, often arrogant, opinions prevail, injustices and inequalities may permeate the education of adolescents. Educators must be wary of tokenism or pejorative representations of those who are different from the mainstream, white, power centered majority.   In our current world climate, differences based on religion or culture can be oversimplified or exaggerated. Now, more than ever, schools for adolescents must set the climate for positive relationships and deeper understanding.

Teachers as Change Agents

Change is hard, and perhaps some communities have not changed as much as I would hope. Matthew Shepard's tragic murder still haunts those concerned about acceptance of gay individuals. We have a family friend, a professional, who had a flourishing practice until members of the small community where he lived learned of his gay lifestyle. Since schools are institutions within the larger community, these societal attitudes impact on the school community.

In his book, *Changing Schools from Within*, Roland Barth (1990) suggests that school communities must establish a vision; what do we want this school to be?

Schools reflect societal influences; thus, they cannot change in isolation. Teachers and schools can be agents of change. We must look to the future. Sergiovanni (1996) and Sarason (1995) remind us that for positive change to occur, all members of the school community and the community at large must have a role in establishing a vision and working toward that vision.

Teachers can be change agents as we go beyond our comfort zone. Seymour Sarason (1990) suggests that schools are systems that have developed resistance to change. Betts (1992) attributes the failure to change to the unwillingness of all educators—professors, administrators, and teachers—to address future societal needs. Schools have experienced success in meeting societal needs of the past; however, schools attempt to "interpret current experiences using old models and metaphors" (38). Sarason (1990) believes that classrooms and school systems are not understandable "unless you flush out the power relationships that inform and control the behavior of everyone in these settings" (7). Critical theorists, from Henry Giroux to Patricia Hinchey, agree.

The impact of educational leaders in developmentally and culturally responsive middle schools is apparent in organizational categories such as grouping, scheduling, and facility usage. Curriculum flexibility is evident in the use of a variety of teaching methods and materials, multiple assessment and evaluation methods, exploratory and interdisciplinary courses, and activities designed to address individual abilities, interests, and talents. Flexibility in programs is developed in the ways that the diverse interest, maturation and intellectual developmental levels, and cultural backgrounds are honored in all aspects of the school community. Moreover, flexibility is found in the multiple opportunities provided for students to work with their peers and adults in the school and community.

If we stay within our comfort zones, in the areas of which we are certain and where we feel safe, little will change. A "healthy skepticism" is important. One should suspect that fundamental assumptions and beliefs may need to be tested, that alternatives should be investigated (McPeck 1992, 42). King and Brownell (1966) caution teachers to avoid reliance on intuition, although intuition can be helpful. The effectiveness of teachers is based upon a thorough knowledge of their subjects, knowledge of their students, knowledge of teaching and learning, and knowledge of their own beliefs and assumptions. One must remember that knowledge about teaching and learning, because the world is ever changing, is not an absolute. Therefore, the search for knowledge is unending and ever changing.

Teachers can expand their knowledge for personal growth in theory and pedagogy by being teacher researchers. By participating in the educational discourse community, they can share this personal understanding of the reality of the classroom with colleagues. Teachers, who are willing to challenge their own assumptions or the situations they observe in their classrooms, can become researchers of their own situations. Too often, the term research is connected with the "ivory tower" or laboratories. Valid research that has meaning for the classroom can and should be conducted by the teachers who live the experience. To become researchers, teachers identify an issue and explore not only the technical aspects of a situation but explore the impact of a situation toward an educational goal. Critical teacher researchers explore the questions of why a situation exists and what social and political conditions influence choices and actions (Noffke and Stevenson 1995).

Joe L. Kincheloe provides guidelines for teachers who are interested in incorporating critical action research into their teaching. First, one should construct a system of meaning and look for philosophical guidance for research and teaching. An understanding of the dominant research methods and their effects, in conjunction with the assumptions of these strategies, combined with the philosophical understanding, builds a foundation for research. Critical action researchers look at familiar settings from many perspectives and look for different research strategies for different situations. After information is collected, the researcher attempts to uncover relationships and patterns that may lead to direction in professional life. With an understanding of theories and assumptions that have guided them, critical action researchers understand how they have been influenced to act and believe the way they do. Finally, critical action researchers look at teaching as a freeing, theory into practice activity (Kincheloe 1991).

We must not be afraid of change and responsibility. Curiosity and creativity must be encouraged. The fact is that schooling children will be different in the twenty-first century. It is troubling to see a trend that may be emerging. Along with the standards and accountability movement, organizations such as the Carnegie Corporation seem to be focusing less on the needs of adolescents in favor of other issues. According to Andrew W. Jackson, a former participant in Carnegie's Council on Adolescent Development, and Gayle A. Davis, a former project director of the Middle Grade School-State Policy Initiative, and others the original *Turning Points* did not complete the work. In their book, *Turning Points 2000: Educating Adolescents for the 21ˢᵗ Century* (2000), the emphasis is on practical applications of information in the original report. Their work resonates with the call to go beyond organizational and structural change and to continue to focus on the elements of a good middle school.

We can't allow old myths to inhibit us. We can't rely on rhetoric. We must engage in serious conversations at all levels of society about what is and what could be. Dick Tracy's wrist communicator is a reality. Astronauts live on space stations for months. So now what will the future bring? We should not be afraid to open the box, make education a priority, take every opportunity to engage others in conversations about learning and schooling, look at issues from all perspectives, encourage curiosity and creativity, take an active role in schooling decisions, and dream and look toward the future.

Becoming Practical

I am known as a nuts and bolts kind of person so at this point it is time for practical suggestions that readers can use to take action. Some of the references provided give the readers specific suggestions that will expand on the ideas presented here. Readers must remember that systemic change takes time. Schools that have made significant changes have spent two or three years in the initial planning stage and then as the school needs changed continued study and activity.

School Wide Change

- Solicit support at the administrative or organizational level when an individual or group of individuals identifies a need. The topics can be raised at departmental or team level meetings at which others who interact with the students can share their perceptions and ideas. Another source of support may be a district wide professional development program. Some schools have study groups designed around particular issues. It may take time to garner the support, and some systems may be resistant at the outset. Nevertheless, enthusiasm is contagious. Organizational support at the beginning will facilitate the success; lack of initial support may delay changes. Persevere.
- Identify a task force and delegate specific responsibilities. Definite roles and responsibilities encourage follow through.
- Continue to expand the network of interested individuals. Talk about what you are learning or studying to anyone who will listen.

- Establish a communication network; a newsletter or website with an email list that will keep people abreast of project progress. Include a way for community members to submit ideas or ask questions.

- Assess current conditions. This includes not only the issues that are pressing in the district but also includes what resources are available such as curriculum, finances, buildings, professional staff, and materials for student use.

- Work with the community. Talk with agencies that have after school programs or work with adolescents. Talk with parent groups who have insights into the needs and concerns of their children. Some communities have foundations dedicated to the support of their schools. These foundations might provide financial support for study materials or meetings. Community involvement will increase the chances for a successful program.

- Work with students. Talk with them about their issues. Involve student organizations such as the student council but do not limit discussions to students who are usually active in school affairs. Talk with students who are not successful or who may be "discipline problems." In addition to personal discussions, schools can use surveys to gather data about student perceptions of their learning environment. There are several good surveys available.

- Work with institutes of higher learning. Education departments will have access to literature and research that may not be easily obtained by individual teachers. Colleges and universities often have access to grant opportunities that involve collaboration between basic and higher education. College students may be involved in gathering information and analyzing data that are gathered during the study.

- Contact professional organizations that may have research reports or information about other school districts that have successfully made the transition to their visions. Be wary though; what works in one district may not work in another.

- Establish a vision. What do we want our school to be? Include all stakeholders in the vision development. Remember to invite parents, community members, school board members, administrators, teachers, students, and any other group that has an influence on the success of the program.

- Continue research and study. Identify specific tasks that need to be done to be successful.

- Look for creative or non-conventional solutions to obstacles. Think of obstacles as opportunities to explore new ideas.
- Identify priorities but realize that systemic change cannot be done piecemeal. Elements of a supportive learning environment do not happen in isolation.
- Create a timeline. Set specific goals and identify the product that will be completed.
- Establish criteria for success. How will we know we have been successful? Consider both academic and social/emotional criteria.
- Provide time for teachers to meet together and plan for the new school environment. Change takes energy and extra time.
- Start slowly. Some tasks can be started with little preparation or effort. Early successes are motivation to continue.
- Reflect and evaluate throughout the process. Learn from mistakes. When something doesn't work, ask why. Did we give the task the necessary support or time? If something worked, also ask why it worked.
- Provide opportunities for teachers and administrators to meet with students and community members to get feedback and suggestions for improvement.
- Share your successes with others. Be proud of the school the community has embraced.

Individual Action

In some cases, individuals may sense a need for change, but they do not find support within their schools or communities. These individuals may still be able to provide a supportive environment within their classrooms. Individuals can use many of the strategies that are effective in school-wide change efforts.

- Reflect upon your own beliefs and assumptions.
- Learn about the community and the students in your classroom.
- Talk to parents and other community members.
- Involve yourself in the school and community.
- Listen to what your students are saying.
- Search for new ideas and colleagues who have similar interests.

- Research information about adolescent issues and middle school philosophy.
- Evaluate your current classroom curriculum and materials.
- Evaluate your current classroom practices.
- Make changes based upon your assessment of the students' needs.
- Set parameters of acceptable behavior.
- Create a communication system to keep in touch with parents and students.
- Be a role model for your students; show respect for your students' ideas and opinions.
- Help students learn to voice their own opinions and respect the opinions of others.
- Model life-long learning.
- Share your successes; when others see your success, they may be curious.

This book was not intended to give all the answers. I do not pretend to have them. Readers of my work may agree or disagree with my positions. Nevertheless if I provoke a conversation, I am successful. In the final chapter of this work, the reader will find an annotated bibliography of books that I have found helpful in my quest toward understanding diversity and my role as a teacher and learner. There were many more books I could have included, and readers may have others they find helpful which they could share with colleagues. As we learn and grow together we can work toward middle schools for a diverse society.

CHAPTER 9

Recommended Reading

It was actually quite hard deciding which books to include in this chapter. There are many that could be included. I finally narrowed my choices to fifteen. I attempted to include a variety of books that present different perspectives from autobiography, critical theory, feminist theory, constructivism, curriculum theory, and research. I also wanted books that addressed issues readers can connect to practical applications. I will share my personal reflections about the books but because readers bring their personal experiences to the material they read, my readers may not interpret the texts in the same manner as I did. That is OK. Hopefully, these books will be a starting point for each reader's professional journey into middle schools for a diverse society. For additional references readers are encouraged to review the extensive bibliography provided at the end of this work.

Brooks, Geraldine. (1995). *Nine Parts of Desire: The Hidden World of Islamic Women*. New York: Anchor Books.

I added this book to my list after reading it as a faculty member in the Scholars Program for students at our college. It provoked discussion among students as they struggled to understand Middle Eastern culture. The text discusses inconsistencies and differences in the Muslim tradition. The author provides a historical perspective that reveals traditions that have emerged in the religion and in political interpretations of the traditions. Students admitted that at times they were shocked and other times they understood the issues facing women behind the veils of their culture.

Crow Dog, Mary and Erdoes, Richard. (1990). *Lakota Woman*. New York: HarperCollins, Publishers.

This autobiography of a Native American woman tells her story from her childhood days living on a reservation through her activist period in the 1970s. She sheds light on traditions that are often misunderstood. Political and power issues within the American society are related to her life. Her words, often bitter, tell of schools that attempt to separate her from her Native American beliefs and her days at the standoff at *Wounded Knee*. I could not put this book down until I had finished it.

Eder, Donna, Evans, Catherine. C., and Parker, Stephen. (1995). *School Talk: Gender and Adolescent Culture*. New Brunswick, NJ: Rutgers University Press.

I found this book by accident in 1996 and have relied on it as a valuable resource for many projects. Since then I have learned that it is used as a reference not only in education courses but also in sociology. Eder and her colleagues spent about two years with middle school students and were able to get an inside view of their lives in school. I was particularly interested in the role that language, words used by teachers and adolescents, had in affecting the relationships and identities of the students.

Giroux, Henry A. (1996). *Fugitive Cultures: Race, Violence, and Youth*. New York: Routledge.

If one knew the background of Henry Giroux, one would not expect him to be a leading educational theorist, author, and distinguished professor at a large university. He beat the odds. In this book, he shares the story of his youth in a working-class neighborhood as the background for his discussion of cultural studies. He sheds light on racial and gender issues as they impact upon youth through mass media. Giroux certainly provoked me to think about things I take for granted.

Harbeck, Karen M. (Editor). (1991). *Coming Out of the Classroom Closet: Gay and Lesbian Students, Teachers, and Curricula.* Binghamton, NY: Harrington Press.

This is a book of essays that explore issues that arise in education at all levels, from pre-school to higher education. I found the article by James Sears, "Educators, Homosexuality, and Homosexual Students: Are Personal Feelings Related to Personal Beliefs?" which directly addressed the adolescent perceptions of the school environment and the perceptions of teachers about the same topic especially thought provoking. Sears also investigated the beliefs of pre-service teachers.

Hart, Elva Traviño. (1999). *Barefoot Heart: Stories of a Migrant Child.* Tempe, AZ: Bilingual Press/Editorial Bilingüe.

In a simple but elegant manner, Elva Traviño Hart tells her story from the migrant farms to the corporate boardrooms. This book was valuable as I prepared Chapter 3 about the development of identity. She shared that mathematics became her vehicle for success; she felt that she could be criticized for her language, but in mathematics there is one right answer, and no one could fault her for her culture. This revelation was helpful in my understanding of student perceptions of curriculum and success. This is a powerful story worthy of rereading.

Hinchey, Patricia H. (1998). *Finding Freedom in the Classroom: A Practical Introduction to Critical Theory.* New York: Peter Lang Publishing.

As the title suggests, Hinchey translates the confusing aspects of critical theory into the vernacular of practicality. She uses autobiographical examples to illustrate the central issues of power and knowledge. The book is intended for those who are encountering critical theory for the first time. It will provide those who are beginning to reflect upon their assumptions and beliefs a framework for thought. It is also valuable for those who struggle with critical theory, as I did in my graduate work. The book will be valuable for those who are beginning their study of developmentally and culturally responsive middle schools and those who are ready to develop a vision and initiate change.

Kohl, Herbert. (1967/1988). *36 Children.* New York: Penguin Books.

I am pleased to find this book still on Education Department reading lists and I recently saw a copy in the hands of a philosophy professor. I had to include this book in this chapter because it made such an impression on me as a young college student. At the time I thought that this story expressed the meaning of teaching and my belief is the same today. This is the true story of a young man who spent a year with a sixth grade class in Harlem in the 1960s. He portrays the struggles for teachers and learners in poor, urban neighborhoods. It is disheartening to realize that situations in urban schools really haven't changed. Nevertheless, the book encourages those who are interested in teaching to look for the creativity and the enthusiasm that may be hidden in the children who are often considered to be failures in traditional educational system.

Kohn, Alfie. (1993/1999). *Punished by Rewards: The Trouble with Gold Stars, Incentive Plans, A's, Praise, and Other Bribes.* New York: Houghton Mifflin Company.

Alfie Kohn challenges behavioristic approaches to motivation. According to Kohn, we are doing our students a disservice by teaching students to learn for a reward instead of learning for learning's sake. He argues that students actually may do less work that is of poorer quality when they are only motivated by rewards. He suggests that the role of schools is to help students work together in learning, evaluate knowledge, and make thoughtful choices. Readers are challenged to reflect upon their beliefs about intrinsic and extrinsic motivation. The book directly relates to Chapter 4, Success, although ideas found in other chapters are also discussed. In addition to extensive theoretical arguments, Kohn also provides practical suggestions for teachers who are attempting to move from a competitive, grade-centered atmosphere to one in which students are involved in a community of learners. The 1998 edition includes an updated afterword by the author. Kohn includes extensive notes and references. This book will certainly provoke discussion among parents, teachers, and community members.

Kottler, Ellen and Kottler, Jeffery A. (2002). *Children with Limited English: Teaching Strategie for the Regular Classroom (Second Edition).* Thousand Oaks, CA: Corwin Press.

This book is definitely a help to pre-service and experienced teachers who are faced with developing a supportive environment for those who are challenged by language diversity. The authors give readers background information about the education of the students including their needs and learning styles. Teachers will find this book to be a valuable resource for teaching strategies. I was particularly interested in the discussion of students who are multilingual.

Ladson-Billings, Gloria. (1994). *The Dreamkeepers: Successful Teachers of African American Children.* San Francisco, CA: Jossey-Bass.

Ladson-Billings tells not only her own story but also the stories of teachers who support students in culturally relevant classrooms. The dedicated teachers she described gave their students hope and urged them to be successful. Even though some of the teachers were not African-American, they sought to meet the needs of their students by understanding the culture of their students and being active participants in the students' communities. She urges readers to reflect upon the ways they teach.

Noddings, Nel. (1992). *The Challenge to Care in Schools: An Alternative Approach to Education.* New York: Teachers College Press.

As I mentioned in Chapter 1, this book was an inspiration early in my studies of young adolescents and schools that support them. I was particularly impressed by the logical way Noddings presented the aspects of care within a school environment. An important concept she presented early in her text was that students need to learn to care about themselves before they can learn to care for others. A supportive teacher is challenged to help her students value their own experiences and self. This circle of care expands from self to others. She also emphasizes that students can learn to care for the ideas and opinions of others. Noddings provides not only theory but practical suggestions for teachers who want to establish an atmosphere of care, respect, and trust in their classrooms.

Noffke, Susan E. and Stevenson, Robert B., Editors. (1995). *Educational Action Research: Becoming Practically Critical.* New York: Teachers College Press.

This book would be especially helpful for teachers who are interested in classroom based teacher research. It clearly explains theoretical bases for such research and gives examples of research that has been done. The book has sections for pre-service teacher education programs as well as for experienced teachers. It also has a section that provides suggestions for administrators who wish to support classroom teachers who are interested in researching their practices to improve instruction and increase positive support for learning in their classroom. The book would be an excellent resource for schools that are embarking on change initiatives as suggested in Chapter 8.

Sergiovanni, Thomas J. (1994). *Building Community in Schools.* San Francisco, CA: Jossey-Bass.

Sergiovanni's book is an excellent foundation for those who are exploring community theory and connections with school practices. He emphasizes the importance of shared values and vision. He gives practical suggestions and examples of schools that have participated in community building activities. The book connects theory to practice in an easy to read format.

Spring, Joel. (2002). *Conflict of Interest: The Politics of American Education (Fourth Edition).* New York: McGraw-Hill.

This is a frank interpretation of the state of American education as the result of powerful economics and political forces. Spring traces major education policy at federal, state, and local levels and the result of this policy on what happens inside the classroom. He identifies sources of conflict about education, knowledge, and power within American society. Of particular interest is the tug of war between conservative and liberal factions as they influence curriculum. I was particularly interested in his description of the political evolution of the standards and assessment movement through the Clinton and Bush administrations.

BIBLIOGRAPHY

Abreu, J. M., R. K. Goodyear, A. Campos, and M.C. Newcomb. 2000. Ethnic belonging and traditional masculinity ideology among African Americans, European Americans and Latinos. *Psychology of Men and Masculinity*, 1(2): 75–86.

Ames, L.B., F. L. Ilg, and S. M. Baker. 1952. *Your ten-to-fourteen year-old*. New York: Dell Publishing.

Anderson, L.W. and R. B. Burns. 1989. *Research in classrooms: The study of teachers, teaching, and instruction*. New York: Pergamon Press.

Anyon, J. 1995. Race, social class, and educational reform in an inner-city school. *Teachers College Record*, 97(1): 69–94.

Apple, M. W. and J. A. Beane. 1995. The case for democratic schools. In *Democratic schools*, edited by M. W. Apple and J. A. Beane. Alexandria, VA: Association for Supervision and Curriculum Development.

Arnot, M. 1994. Male hegemony, social class, and women's education. In *The education feminist reader*, edited by L. Stone (with G. G. Boldt). New York: Routledge.

Ascher, C. 1989. Southeast Asian adolescents: Identity and adjustment. EERIC/CUE Digest 51. ED 306329.

Associated Press. 2001. Award winning book frequent target in schools. (cited 1-12-03). Available online: www.freedomforum.org/templates/document.asp?documentID=14344.

Ausubel, D. P. 1968. *Educational psychology: A cognitive view*. New York: Holt, Rinehart, and Winston.

Ayers, W. 1990. Small heroes: In and out of school with 10-year old city kids. *Cambridge Journal of Education*, 20(3): 269–276.

Banathy, B. H. 1996. Conversation in social system design. *Educational Technology*, 36(1): 39-41.

Barnes, G. G. 1996. Gender issues. In *The voice of the child: Handbook for professionals*, edited by R. Davie, G. Upton, and V. Varma. Bristol, PA: The Falmer Press, Taylor & Francis, Inc.

Barth, R. S. 1990. *Improving schools from within: Teachers, parents, and principals can make a difference.* San Francisco: Jossey-Bass.

Bartolomé, L. I. 1997. Mismatched classroom discourse. *Taboo,* I: 167–198.

Battistich, V., D. Solomon, D. Kim, M. Watson, and E. Schaps. 1995. Schools as communities, poverty levels of student populations, and students' attitudes, motives, and performance: A multilevel analysis. *American Educational Research Journal,* 32 (3): 627–658.

Beane, J. A. 1992. Turning the floor over: Reflections on a middle school curriculum. *Middle School Journal,* 23(3): 34–40.

———. 1993. *A Middle school curriculum: From rhetoric to reality.* Columbus, OH: National Middle School Association.

Belenky, M. F., B.V. Clinchy, N. R. Goldberger, and J. M. Tarule. 1986. *Women's way of knowing.* New York: Basic Books.

Berger, K. S. (with R. A. Thompson). 1991. *The developing person through childhood and adolescence.* New York: Worth Publishers.

Bergmann, S. and J. Baxter. 1983. Building a guidance program and advisory concept for early adolescents. *NASSP Bulletin,* 67 (463): 49–55.

Betts, F. 1992. How systems thinking applies to education. *Educational Leadership,* 50 (3): 38–41.

Blos, P. 1962. *On adolescence: A psychoanalytic approach.* New York: The Free Press.

Bowers, R. S. 1995. Early adolescent social and emotional development: A constructivist perspective. In *Educating young adolescents: Life in the middle,* edited by M. J. Wavering. New York: Garland Publishing, Inc.

Braddock , J. A., II and J. M. McPartland. 1993. Education of early adolescents. *Review of Research in Education,* 19: 135–170.

Brady, J. 1995. *Schooling young children: A feminist pedagogy for liberatory learning.* Albany, NY: State University of New York Press.

Branch, C. W. 2001. The many faces of self: Ego and ethnic identities. *Journal of Genetic Psychology,* 162(4): 412–429.

Brantlinger, E. 1993. Adolescents' interpretations of social class influences on schooling. *The Journal of Classroom Interaction,* 28(1): 1–12.

Brooks, G. 1995. *Nine parts of desire: The hidden world of Islamic women.* New York: Anchor Books.

Brough, J. A. 1990. Changing conditions for young adolescents: Reminiscences and realities. *Educational Horizons,* 68(2): 78–81.

———. 1995. Middle level education: A historical perspective. In *Educating young adolescents: Life in the middle,* edited by M. J. Wavering. New York: Garland Publishing, Inc.

Buck, C. A. 2002. Teaching discourses: Science teachers' responses to the voices of adolescent girls. *Learning Environments Research,* 5(1): 24–50.

Burns, C. 1998. Interracial relationships: What is the color of love? (cited on 4-18-2000). Available online: http://family.go.com/Features/family_1998_04/kids/kids48race/.

Burt, J. M. and G. Halpin. 1998. African American identity development: A review of literature. Paper presented at the meeting of the Mid-south Educational Research Association. November. New Orleans, LA.

California Department of Education. 2002. *Grade seven history—Social science content standards: World history and geography—Medieval and early modern times.* (cited 12-18-02) Available online: http://www.cde.ca.gov/standards/history/grade7.html.

Cannon, J. R. 1995. Further validation of the constructivist learning environment survey: Its use in elementary science methods courses. *Journal of Elementary Science Education,* 7(1): 47–62.

Cantor, L. 1979. *Assertive discipline: A take charge approach for today's educator.* Los Angeles, CA: Cantor and Associates.

Carnegie Council on Adolescent Development. 1989. *Turning points: Preparing American youth for the 21st century.* New York: Carnegie Corporation.

———. 1998. *Great transitions: Preparing adolescents for a new century.* New York: Carnegie Corporation.

Chamberlain, G. K. 1999. *Student perceptions of their middle school learning environment.* Ph.D. diss. The Pennsylvania State University.

Citizens for Excellence in Education. 2003. *Your reliable source on public education.* (cited on 1-05-03). Available online: www.nace-cee.org/ceestrategy.htm.

Cleary, L. M. and T. D. Peacock. 1998. *Collected wisdom: American Indian education.* Needham, MA: Allyn and Bacon.

Cochran-Smith, M. 1995. Color blindness and basket making are not the answers: Confronting race, culture, and language diversity. *American Educational Research Journal,* 32(3): 493–522.

Crick, B. 1999. The presuppositions of citizenship education. *Journal of Philosophy of Education of Great Britain,* 33(3): 337–352.

Davies, M. A. 1995. Age-appropriate teaching strategies. In *Educating young adolescents: Life in the middle,* edited by M. J. Wavering. New York: Garland Publishing, Inc.

Davis, H. A. 2001. The quality and impact of relationships between elementary school students and teachers. *Contemporary Educational Psychology,* 26: 431–453.

Deffenbacher, J. L. and R. C. Swaim. 1999. Anger expression in Mexican-American and White Non-Hispanic adolescents. *Journal of Counseling Psychology,* 46(1): 61–69.

Dewey, J. 1916. *Democracy and education: An introduction to the philosophy of education.* New York: The Macmillan Company.

Dog, M. C. and R. Erdoes. 1990. *Lakota woman.* New York: HarperCollins, Publisher.

Dwivedi, K. N. 1996. Race and the child's perspective. In *The voice of the child: A handbook for professionals,* edited by R. Davie, G. Upton, and V. Varma. Bristol, PA: Falmer Press, Francis & Taylor, Inc.

Eckert, P. 1989. *Jocks and burnouts: Social categories and identity in the high school.* New York: Teachers College Press.

Eder, D. (with C. Evans and S. Parker). 1995. *School talk: Gender and adolescent culture.* New Brunswick, NJ: Rutgers University Press.

Elkind, D. 1984. *All grown up and no place to go: Teenagers in crisis.* New York: Addison Wesley Longman.

Entwisle, D. R., K. L. Alexander, and L. S. Olson. 1997. *Children, schools, and inequality.* Boulder, CO: Westview Press.

Erikson, E. H. 1963/1998. *Childhood and society (35th anniversary edition).* New York: W. W. Norton and Company, Inc.

Estomin, L. 2002. *No justice, no peace.* Video. New York: Filmakers Library.

Fand, F. 1996. Adopt-a-grandparent program teaches about life. *Middle School Journal,* 27(5): 22–28.

Farrell, E. 1990. *Hanging in and dropping out.* New York: Teachers College Press.

154   Middle Schools for a Diverse Society

Fine, M. 1993. You can't just say that the only ones who can speak are those who agree with your position: Political discourse in the classroom. *Harvard Educational Review*, 63(4): 412–433.

Forrest, K. D. 2002. Voiceless: The effect of unfair procedures on recipients and observers in small groups. *Current Research in Social Psychology*, 8(5): 62–83.

Fraser, B. J. 1990. *Individualised classroom environment questionnaire: Handbook and test master set*. Melbourne, Australia: Council for Educational Research, Inc.

———. 1994. Research on classroom and school climate. In *Handbook on science teaching and learning*, edited by D. L. Gabriel, 493–531. New York: MacMillan Publishing Company.

Furtwengler, W. J. 1991. Reducing student misbehavior through student involvement in school restructuring processes. Paper presented at the Annual Conference of the American Association for Educational Research, April. Chicago, IL.

Gardner, H. 1991. *The unschooled mind: How children think and how schools should teach*. New York: Basic Books.

George, P. S. and W. M. Alexander. 1993. *The exemplary middle school (Second Edition)*. Columbus, OH: National Middle School Association.

George, P. S. and K. Shewey. 1994. *New evidence for the middle school*. Columbus, OH: National Middle School Association.

George, P. S., C. Stevenson, J. Thomas, and J. Beane. 1992. *The middle school—And beyond*. Alexandria, VA: Association for Supervision and Curriculum Development.

Gersch, I. S. (with S. Moyse, A. Nolan, and G. Pratt). 1996. Listening to children in educational contexts. In *The voice of the child: A handbook for professionals* edited by R. Davie, G. Upton, and V. Varma. Bristol, PA: The Falmer Press, Taylor and Francis, Inc.

Gilligan, C. 1982. *In a different voice: Psychological theory and women's development*. Cambridge, MA: Harvard University Press.

Giroux, H. J. 1996. *Fugitive cultures: Race, violence, and youth*. New York: Routledge.

Glasser, W. 1998. *Choice theory in the classroom (Revised Edition)*. New York: HarperCollins.

Goleman, D. 1999. *Emotional intelligence: Why it can matter more than IQ*. New York: Bantam Books.

Goyette, K. and Y. Xie. 1999. Educational expectations of Asian American youths: Determinants and ethnic differences. *Sociology of Education*, 72: 22–36.

Graham, J. A., R. Cohen, and S. M. Zbikowski. 1998. A longitudinal investigation of race and sex as factors in children's classroom friendship choices. *Child Study Journal*, 28(4): 245–266.

Gresson, A. D., III. 1997. Identity, class and teacher education. The persistence of "class effect" in the classroom. *Educational Pedagogy and Cultural Studies*, 19(3). Author's copy.

Harbeck, K. (Editor). 1991. *Coming out of the classroom closet: Gay and lesbian students, teachers and curricula*. Binghamton, NY: Harrington Press.

Hart. E. T. 1999. *Barefoot heart: Stories of a migrant child*. Tempe, AZ: Bilingual Press/Editorial Bilingüe.

Havighurst, R. J. 1952. *Developmental tasks and education (Second Edition)*. New York: David McKay Company, Inc.

Herr, K. 1996. Creating safe spaces in middle schools for the voices of girls and women. *Middle School Journal*, 27(5): 16–21.

Hinchey, P. H. 1998. *Finding freedom in the classroom: A practical introduction to critical theory*. New York: Peter Lang.

Holcomb-McCoy, C. C. 1997. Who am I? The ethnic identity development of adolescents. Paper presented at the 1997 American School Counselors Association Conference, June-July. Nashville, TN.

Hom, H. L. 1996. Sports participation and withdrawal: A developmental motivational commentary. *Research in Middle Level Education Quarterly*, 19(2): 41–61.

Huang, G. 1993. Beyond cultures: Communicating with Asian American children and families. ERIC Digest 94, EDO-UD-98-3.

Irvine, J. J. 1986. Teacher-student interactions: Effect of student race, sex, and grade level. *Journal of Educational Psychology*, 78(1): 14–21.

Jackson, A. W., G. A. Davis, M. Abeel, and A. Bordonaro.. 2000. *Turning points 2000: Educating Adolescents for the 21st century*. New York: Teachers College Press.

James, M. 1995. Philosophy: A guide to middle school program development. In *Educating young adolescents: Life in the middle*, edited by M. J. Wavering. New York: Garland Publishing, Inc.

Jenlink, P. and A. A. Carr (Galley proofs). January/February 1996. Conversation as a medium for change in education. *Educational Technology*. 36:31–8.

Jonassen, D. H. 1994. Thinking technology: Toward a constructivist design model. *Educational Technology*, 34(4): 34–37.

Kaba, M. 2001. "They listen to me...but they don't act on it": Contradictory consciousness and student participation in decision making. *High School Journal*, 84(2): 21–34.

Kincheloe, J. L. 1991. *Teachers as researchers: Qualitative inquiry as a path to empowerment*. New York: Falmer Press.

King, A. R. and J. A. Brownell. 1966. *The curriculum and disciplines of knowledge*. New York: Routledge.

Kjos, B. 1996. *Brave New Schools*. Eugene, OR: Harvest Home Publishers, Inc.

Kohl, H. 1967/1988. *36 children*. New York: Penguin Books.

Kohn, A. 1996. *Beyond discipline: From compliance to community*. Alexandria, VA: Association for Supervision and Curriculum Development.

———. 1993/1999. *Punished by rewards: The trouble with gold stars, incentive plans, A's, praise, and other bribes*. New York: Houghton Mifflin Company.

Kohlberg, L. 1981. *The philosophy of moral development: Moral stages and the idea of justice*. San Francisco: Harper & Row.

Kottler, E. and J. A. Kottler. 2002. *Children with limited English: Teaching strategies for the regular classroom (Second Edition)*. Thousand Oaks, CA: Corwin Press.

Kozol, J. 1991. *Savage inequalities: Children in America's schools*. New York: Crown Publishers, Inc.

Ladson-Billings, G. 1994. *The dreamkeepers: Successful teachers of African American children*. San Francisco, CA: Jossey-Bass Publishers.

———. 1995. Toward a theory of culturally relevant pedagogy. *American Educational Research Journal*, 32(3): 465–491.

Langdon, C. A. 1997. The fourth Phi Delta Kappan poll of teachers' attitudes toward public schools. *Phi Delta Kappan*, 79(3): 212–222.

Lewin, K. 1951. *Field theory in social science*. New York: Harper & Brothers.

Lincoln, Y. S. 1989. Critical requisites for transformational leadership: Needed research and discourse. *Peabody Journal of Education*, 66(3): 176–181.

Loewen, J. E. (1996). *Lies my teacher told me: Everything your American history textbook got wrong.* New York: Simon and Schuster.

Lounsbury, J. H. and D. C. Clark. 1990. *Inside grade eight: From apathy to excitement.* Reston, VA: National Association of Secondary School Principals.

Lowery, L. 1993. *The Giver.* New York: Bantam Books.

Manning, M. L. 1993. Cultural and gender differences in young adolescents. *Middle School Journal,* 25(1): 13–17.

Maxwell, T. W. and A. R. Thomas. 1991. School climate and school culture. *Journal of Educational Administration,* 29(2): 72–82.

Maynard, G. 1986. The reality of diversity at the middle level. *Clearing House,* 60(1): 21–23.

McLaughlin, B. and B. McLeod. 1996. Educating all our students: Improving education for children from culturally and linguistically diverse backgrounds. *Final Report of the National Center for Research on Cultural Diversity and Second Language Learning, Volume 1.* Santa Cruz: University of California at Santa Cruz.

McNeely, C. A., J. M. Nonnemaker, and R. W. Blum. 2002. Promoting school connectedness: evidence for the National Longitudinal Study of Adolescent Health. *Journal of School Health,* 72(4): 138–147.

McPeck, J. E. 1992. Teaching critical reasoning through the disciplines: Content versus process. In *Critical reasoning in contemporary culture,* edited by R. A. Talask. Albany: State University of New York Press.

McRobbie, A. 1991. *Feminism and youth culture: From Jackie to just seventeen.* Cambridge, MA: Unwin Hyman, Inc.

Mead, M. 1961/1973. *Coming of age in Samoa.* New York: William Morrow & Company.

Mills, R. F. 1995. Preparing teachers for middle level schools: Meeting the needs of the adolescents. In *Educating young adolescents: Life in the middle,* edited by M. J. Wavering. New York: Garland Publishing, Inc.

Mitchell, S. A. and M. V. Black. 1995. *Freud and beyond: A history of modern psychoanalytical thought.* New York: Basic Books.

Moos, R. 1976. *The human context: Environmental determinants of behavior.* New York: Wiley.

———. 1991. Connections between school, work and family settings. In *Educational environments: Evaluation, antecedents, and consequences,* edited by B. J. Fraser and H. Walberg. Oxford, New York: Pergamon Press.

Muus, R. E. 1982. *Theories of adolescence (Fourth Edition).* New York: Random House, Inc.

NASSP's Council on Middle Level Education. 1989. *Middle level education's responsibility for intellectual development.* Reston, VA: National Association of Secondary School Principals.

———. 1993. *Achieving excellence through middle level education.* Reston, VA: National Association of Secondary School Principals.

National Middle School Association (NMSA). 1995. *This we believe–Developmentally responsive middle level schools.* Columbus, OH: Author.

Nieto, S. 1994. Lessons from students on creating a chance to dream. *Harvard Educational Review,* 64(4): 392–426.

Noddings, N. 1992. *The challenge to care in schools: An alternative approach to education.* New York: Teachers College Press.

————. 1995. A morally defensible mission for schools in the 21st century. *Phi Delta Kappan*, 76(5): 365–368.

Noffke, S. E. and R. B. Stevenson. (Editors). 1995 *Educational action research: Becoming practically critical.* New York: Teachers College Press.

Northwest Regional Educational Laboratory (NWREL). 2002. *Improving black student achievement.* (cited on 8-25-02). Available online: http://www.nwrel.org/cnornse/booklets/achieve/1.html.

Oakes, J., A. Vasudeva and M. Jones. 1996. Becoming educative: Reforming curriculum and teaching in the middle grades. *Research in Middle Level Education Quarterly*, 20(1): 11–40.

O'Connor, C. 1999. Race, class, and gender in America: Narrative of opportunity among American low-income African American youths. *Sociology of Education*, 72: 137–157.

Ogbu, J. U. 1992. Adaptation to minority status and impact on school success. *Theory into Practice*, 31(4): 287–295.

O'Neil, J. 1998. Why are all the black kids sitting together? A conversation with Beverly Daniel Tatum. *Educational Leadership*, 55(4): 12–17.

Osher, D. and B. Mejia. 1999. Overcoming barriers to intercultural relationship: A culturally competent approach. *Reaching Today's Youth*, 3(2): 48–52.

Peña, R. A. 1997. Cultural differences and the construction of meaning: Implications for the leaderships and organization context of schools. *Education Policy Analysis Archives*, 5(10). (cited on 7-17-00). Available online: http://olam.ed.aus.edu/epaa/v5n10.html

Phinney. J. S. 1989. Stages of ethnic identity in minority group adolescents. *Journal of Early Adolescence*, 9: 34–49.

Phinney, J. S. and N. J. Cobb. 1996. Reasoning about intergroup relations among Hispanic and Euro-American adolescents. *Journal of Adolescent Research*, 11(3): 306–324.

Pinar, W. F., W. M. Reynolds, P. Slattery and P. M. Taubaum. 1995. *Understanding curriculum.* New York: Peter Lang.

Pipher, M. 1994. *Reviving Ophelia: Saving the selves of adolescent girls.* New York: Ballentine Books.

Pollack, W. 1998. *Real boys: Rescuing our sons from the myths of boyhood.* New York: Henry Holt and Company.

Pollack, W. (with T. Shuster). 2000. *Real boys' voices.* New York: Random House.

Reed, B. and C. Russell. 1995. Leadership in middle level schools. In *Educating young adolescents: Life in the middle*, edited by M. J. Wavering. New York: Garland Publishing, Inc.

Renchler, R. 2000. Grade span. *Research Roundup, National Association of Elementary School Principals*, 16(3).

Resnick, M. D., L. J. Harris, and R. W. Blum. 1993. The impact of caring and connectedness on adolescent health and well-being. *Children, Youth, and Family Consortium.* (cited on 11-6-02). Available online: www.cyfcumn.edu/adolescents/resources/caring.html.

Rice, F. P. 1999. *The adolescent: Development, relationships, and culture (Ninth Edition).* Boston, MA: Allyn and Bacon.

Robertson, E. 1996. Response to: Teacher authority and teaching for liberations. Available online: http://www/ed/uiud/edi/coe/eps.pes-yarbook/94docs/robers.htm.

Robertson, P. 1991. *Brave new world.* Nashville, TN: Word Publishing, Inc.

Sadker, M. and D. Sadker. 1994. *Failing at fairness: How America's schools cheat girls.* New York: Charles Scribner's Sons.

Saporito, S. and A. Lareau. 1999. In framing educational choice. *Social Problems,* 46(3): 418–439.

Sarason, S. B. 1990. *The predictable failure of educational reform: Can we change course before it's too late?* San Francisco, CA: Jossey-Bass.

Schmuck, R. A. and P. Schmuck, M. 2001. *Group processes in the classroom.* New York: McGraw-Hill Higher Education.

Schockley, R., R. Schumacher, and D. Smith 1989. Teacher advisory programs: Strategies for successful implementation. *NASSP Bulletin,* 68(473): 69–74.

Sergiovanni, T. J. 1992. Why we should seek substitutes for leadership. *Educational Leadership,* 49(5): 41–45.

———. 1994. *Building community in school.* San Francisco, CA: Jossey-Bass.

———. 1996. *Leadership for the schoolhouse: How is it different? Why is it important?* San Francisco, CA: Jossey-Bass.

Shor, I. 1992. *Empowering education: Critical teaching for social change.* Chicago, IL: University of Chicago Press.

———. 1996. *When students have power: Negotiating authority in a critical pedagogy.* Chicago, IL: University of Chicago Press.

Sizer, T. R. 1992. *Horace's school: Redesigning the American high school* Boston, MA: Houghton Mifflin.

Slattery, P. 1995. *Curriculum development in the postmodern era.* New York: Garland Publishing, Inc.

Slavin, R. E. 1994. *Educational psychology: Theory and practice.* Needham Heights, MA: Allyn and Bacon.

Sleeter, C. E. and C. A. Grant. 1987. An analysis of multicultural education in the United States. *Harvard Educational Review,* 57(4): 421–440.

Smith, B. 1995. Transcending classroom management: Assisting the development of caring, responsibility, and community in the middle school classroom. In *Educating young adolescents: Life in the middle,* edited by M. J. Wavering. New York: Garland Publishing, Inc.

Spencer, M. S., L. D. Icard, T. W. Harachi, R. F. Catalano, and M. Oxford. 2000. Ethnic identity among monoracial and multiracial early adolescence. *Journal of Early Adolescence,* 20(4): 365–387.

Spring, J. 2002. *Conflict of interest: The politics of American education (Fourth Edition).* New York: McGraw-Hill.

Strodl, P. 1997. Teachers who become leaders. (cited on 3-14-1997). Available online: http://www.coe.usouthal.edu/faculty/peter_strodl.leading.htm

Strough, J. and C. Berg. 2000. Goals as a mediator of gender differences in high affiliation dyadic conversations. *Developmental Psychology,* 36(1): 117–125.

Sulentic, M. 2001. Black English in a place called Waterloo. *Multicultural Education,* 8(4): 24-30.

Talbot, M. 2002. Men behaving badly. *The New York Times Magazine,* October 13: 52–57+.

Taylor, P., V. Dawson, and B. Fraser. 1995. Classroom learning environment: A constructivist perspective. Paper presented at the annual meeting of the American Educational Research Association (AERA). April. San Francisco, CA.

Thorne, B. 1992. Girls and boys together…but mostly apart: Gender arrangements in elementary schools. In *Education and gender equity,* edited by J. Wrigley. Bristol, PA: The Falmer Press.

Thurlow, C. 2001. Naming the "outsider within": Homophobic pejoratives and the verbal abuse of lesbian, gay, and bisexual high-school pupils. *Journal of Adolescence,* 24: 25–38.

Bibliography 159

Tyler, R. W. 1949. *Basic principals of curriculum and instruction*. Chicago, IL: University of Chicago Press.

Uribe, V. and K. M. Harbeck. 1992. Addressing the needs of lesbian, gay and bisexual youth: The origins of PROJECT 10 and school-based interventions. In *Coming out of the classroom closet*, edited by K. M. Harbeck. New York: Harrington Press.

US Department of Commerce. 1998. *Census Brief: Children without health insurance*. CEMBR/98-1. Available online: http://www.census.gov/prod/www/abs/briefs/html.

US Department of Education. 2002. *Title I- Improving the Academic Achievement of the Disadvantaged*. (cited on 11-15-02). Available online: http://www.ed.gov/legislation/ESEA02/pg2. html.

Vars, G. 1997. Student concerns and standards too. *Middle School Journal*, 28(4): 44–49.

Walker, D. M. and C. D. Lirgg. 1995. Growth and development through the middle school years. In *Educating young adolescents: Life in the middle* edited by M. J. Wavering. New York: Garland Publishing, Inc.

Walkerdine, V. 1994. Femininity as performance. In *The education feminist reader,* edited by L. Stone (with G. M. Boldt). New York: Routledge.

Wardle, F. 1992. Supporting biracial children in the school setting. *Education and Treatment of Children,* 15(2): 163–172.

Weiler, K. 1991. Freire and a feminist pedagogy of difference. *Harvard Educational Review,* 61(4): 449–469.

Weissert, W. 1999. Report cites racial gap in student performance. *The Chronicle of Higher Education* 46(10): A42.

Williamson, R. and J. H. Johnston. Through the looking glass: The future of middle level education. (cited on 12-11-1996). Available online: http://nassp.org:80/SERVICES/Future.htm

Wolfolk A. E. 1998. *Educational psychology (Seventh Edition)*. Boston, MA: Allyn and Bacon.

INDEX

A

Ability 9, 23, 26, 34, 46, 50 67, 72,
    86, 98, 103, 122
  cognitive 16, 44, 69
  intellectual 26
Abstract thinking 44, 45, 57, 69
Academic 6, 16, 17, 34, 41, 46, 50, 57,
    59, 61–63, 66, 67, 117
  achievement 14, 37,44, 45, 56, 57,
    69
  success 61, 63–65, 68, 69
Acceptance 18, 30, 31, 43, 49, 50, 61,
    78, 79, 99
  peer 61
Accountability 118, 130, 134
Achievement 23, 25, 45, 50, 57, 60–
    62, 69, 70, 78, 81, 89, 110, 120,
    134, 135
  academic 14, 37, 44, 45, 56, 57, 69
  identity 41, 48
Acting white 48, 87

Action 113, 114, 119, 125
  research 130
  social 11, 12, 33, 67
Activities, competitive 62, 83
Activism, political 8
Administrative 6, 14, 81, 119, 139
Administrator[s] 9, 31, 35, 58, 81, 93–
    95, 99, 108, 118–120, 131, 137,
    140, 141, 148
Adolescent
  beliefs 42
  development 6, 12, 21, 22, 24, 28-30
  needs 12, 17, 19, 22–24, 28, 30, 31
    37, 137, 30
Advisory 6, 41, 81, 90, 132
African American identity 46, 49, 53
Aggressive 82, 83, 88, 89
Alexander, William 30
Algebra 44
Anger 8, 14, 15, 105–107
Anthropology, cultural 25, 29
Appearance 62, 66, 67, 84

Appropriate, developmentally 6, 12, 24,
    32, 56, 70, 134
Approval, peer 4
Asian 11, 50, 64, 132
Asian students 65, 133
Assessment 33, 68–70, 110, 130, 137,
    150
Assimilation 11, 13, 22, 87
Assertive Discipline 104
Association for Supervision and
    Curriculum Development 28
Association of Teacher Educators 127
Assumptions 7, 11, 18, 19, 21, 23, 27,
    32, 36, 40, 50, 56, 76, 77, 82, 89,
    93, 96, 99, 121, 123, 125, 137,
    138, 141, 145
Athletics 83
Attitudes 6, 32, 40, 41, 48, 49, 53, 57,
    60, 63, 64, 66, 70, 79, 80, 83, 85,
    93, 105
    societal 136
    teacher 32, 40, 53

B

Background[s] 7, 17, 23, 29, 17, 50,
    59, 78, 92, 133
    cultural 26, 28, 48, 63, 66, 86
    economic 50
Banks, James 49
Barefoot Heart: Stories of a Migrant Child 47
Barriers 10, 87, 87, 114, 123, 125
    success 10
Barth, Roland 37
Beane, James 30, 125
Behavior 16, 24, 26, 28, 30, 33, 34,
    44, 45, 52, 53, 63, 65, 90, 102,
    103, 106, 137, 142

competitive 63, 82, 83
Belenky, Mary 36
Belief[s] 7, 14, 16, 19, 33, 36, 42, 67,
    76, 92, 95, 97–102, 123, 125, 137,
    141
    adolescent 42
    cultural 85
    immigrant 64
    parent 48, 100
    student 50, 79, 86, 88, 109, 123
    teacher 115
    system 94
Belong 10, 11, 14, 57, 65, 84, 93, 120
Belonging 47, 77–80, 87
Bias[es] 11, 18, 29 30, 51, 76, 82, 83,
    112, 125, 133
    gender 51
Bilingual 68, 133
Biracial 15, 50, 133
    children 15
    identity 50
    literature 15
    marriage 15, 49
    students 49
Black student identity 49
Blos, Peter 25, 28
Body image 25, 40, 43
Body language 119
Boys 42, 45, 51, 52, 62, 80–84, 112,
    123, 125
Brown v. Board of Education 127
Bruton Heights School 127
Business 18, 51, 57, 104, 124, 130,
    135

C

Capital, cultural 18, 67

Care 6, 7, 18, 29, 30, 33, 40, 43, 48, 53, 56, 59, 71, 114, 116, 122, 125, 147

Caring 7, 31, 32, 56, 65, 65, 80, 81, 97

Carnegie Corporation 138

Carnegie Council 8, 18, 19, 27, 28, 31, 32, 35, 41, 56, 67, 69, 70, 91, 94, 115, 124, 131, 138

Certification, teacher 23, 135

Challenges 6, 10, 12, 13, 16, 18, 19, 21, 24, 32–34, 36-38, 41, 48, 53, 55, 66, 68, 76, 72, 89,95, 125

Challenge to Care in Schools, The 6, 53

Change 5, 6, 12, 14, 24, 34–37, 41, 53, 65-67, 112, 119, 121, 122, 125, 128, 130, 136, 137, 139

organizational 139

Change agents 136, 137

Changing Schools from Within 37

Children
biracial 15
multiracial 12

Children with Limited English 68

Choice 25, 29, 33, 44, 51, 67, 71, 79, 96, 103, 133, 135, 136

Chronic poor 17

Citizenship 32–35, 90, 92, 96, 101, 107, 108

Civil rights 8, 23

Class, social 11, 36, 50, 79, 88, 123

Classroom[s] 9, 12–14, 15–17, 22, 23 32, 34, 41, 43, 45, 46, 49, 52, 53, 61, 62, 65, 68, 71, 72, 80, 85, 97, 102–105, 119, 123, 138, 142

climate 33

environment 21, 41

management 103, 104

practices 14, 15, 103, 104

Climate
classroom 33
political 87
school 30, 35, 90, 124

Cliques 78

Clubs 81

Cognitive abilities 16, 44, 69

Cognitive development 13, 32, 42, 43, 69

Collaboration 67, 81, 118, 119

Columbus 102

Comfort zone 116, 137

Communication 36, 65, 80, 90, 91, 96,97, 108, 110, 112, 114–116, 118, 125, 132, 137, 142
network 140
nonverbal 114

Community 8, 9, 18, 22, 30, 33, 35, 36, 38, 41, 47, 48, 50, 59, 63, 68, 92, 94–98, 100–102, 106–108
democratic 108
global 15
learners 18, 36, 93, 94, 97, 124, 146
learning 18, 21, 31, 33, 35, 36, 53, 92, 97, 103, 124
organizations 97
school 16, 19, 34, 36, 53, 65, 72, 87, 94, 95, 99, 100, 102, 103, 115
service 97, 100–102
supportive 37, 93, 114, 134
theory 7, 98, 130, 148

Competition 34, 61, 62, 55, 58, 76

Competitive
activities 62, 83
behaviors 63, 82, 83

Competitiveness 34, 59, 63

Concept, middle school 22, 23, 31
Concrete thinking 44, 57, 69
Conference, parent 6, 17, 18, 68, 113,
    115, 116, 155
Confidential[ity], 121, 122
Conflict 26, 29, 40, 62, 63, 67, 111,
    134
Consensus 11, 102, 125, 128, 134
Consequences 92, 96, 102
Constructivist 36, 37, 56, 71, 79, 82,
    93, 94, 98, 99, 130
Control 33, 34, 49, 59, 60, 76, 98,
    103
Controversy 11, 61, 98, 111
Controversial issues 108
Cooperation 35, 59, 72, 76
Cooperative learning 11, 64, 80, 83, 86,
    111, 122, 123
Creativity 42, 61
Critical
  action research 138
  theory 37, 130, 137, 145
  thinking 118, 129
Criticism 43, 51, 61, 86, 104, 112
Criticism of schools 118
Cross-race friendships 85
Cultural 7, 11, 24–26, 28, 37, 41, 46,
    45, 48, 53, 61, 63-65, 67, 84
  anthropology 25, 28
  backgrounds 26, 28, 48, 63, 66, 86
  beliefs 85
  capital 18, 67
  differences 7, 26, 46, 72, 121, 136
  diversity 26, 41, 46, 53, 64, 67
  expectations 45, 46, 84
  experiences 113
  factors 106
  frame of reference 63, 67, 68

  groups 11, 64, 48
  identity 47, 67
  images 66
  influences 24, 36
  interpretations 80
  mistrust 86
  norms 63
  perspective 59, 65
  pluralism 11
Culturally 25, 28, 29
  relevant 63, 86–88, 132, 134, 147
  responsive 68, 75, 76, 87, 88, 96,
      99, 105, 108, 109, 111, 117,
      133, 135, 146
Culture 27, 37
  dominant 11, 17, 22, 48, 49, 53, 64,
      67, 68, 99, 124
  school 123
  wars 98
  youth 42, 81, 94, 124
Curriculum 6, 7, 11, 13, 22, 30, 37 36,
    41, 42, 44, 48, 53, 66–70, 96, 101,
    102, 118, 120, 122, 124, 132, 133,
    136, 137, 140, 142, 145
  theory 9

                    D

Dating 46, 84
Decision 13, 14, 22, 33
  moral 13
Decision making 62, 78, 87, 89, 93,
    94–96, 101, 104, 106
  democratic 131
  group 81
Deconstructionism 36
Democracy 92, 93, 96, 99, 102, 103

Democratic
  community 108
  decision making 131
  schools 63, 92, 103
  society 95, 99
Derrida, Jacques 36
Development[al] 6, 12, 13, 24–28, 37,
  41-45, 53, 78
  adolescent 6, 12, 21, 22, 24, 27–30
  cognitive 13, 32, 42, 43, 69
  emotional 12, 30, 32, 42–44
  identity 25, 29, 33-35, 45–47, 49,
    50, 53, 64, 72, 92
  intellectual 12, 30, 43, 44, 80
  moral 12, 13, 29, 30
  middle school 21, 23
  needs 12, 22, 24, 31, 63, 69, 70
  personal 34, 35, 56
  physical 12, 30, 32, 42–44
  psycho-social 28, 30, 43
  social 12, 30, 43
  theories of 24, 27–30, 45, 131
Developmentally
  appropriate 6, 12, 24, 32, 56, 70,
    134
  responsive 30, 32, 35, 37, 42, 47,
    53, 70, 99, 105, 108, 109, 111,
    121, 137
Dewey, John 36, 93, 128, 129
Dialect 9, 14
Dialogue 18, 35,36, 90,93, 106, 108–
  110, 115, 117, 118, 121, 124
Differences 25–28, 30, 46, 112, 121
  cultural 7, 26, 46, 72, 121, 136
  gender 45, 72, 112, 113, 131
  socio-economic 46, 131
Differentiated 57, 131
  instruction 105

  materials 134
  methods 134
Digital divide 136
Discipline 81, 102, 103
Discrimination 8, 9, 100, 128
Divers [ity] 7–10, 15, 16, 18, 32, 33,
  37, 44. 53, 67, 76, 87, 95, 134
  cultural 26, 41, 46, 53, 64, 67
  economic 16
  ethnic 15
  issues 7, 9, 12, 18
  linguistic 14, 46, 67, 68
  racial 15, 44, 85
  religious 8, 10, 14
  student 48, 53, 67, 85, 131, 132
Dominant
  culture 11, 17, 22, 48, 49, 53, 64,
    67, 68, 99, 124
  group 87
Dreamkeepers: Successful Teachers of African
  American Children, The 53

E

Economic 7–10, 13, 14, 16–18, 21–
  23, 37, 44–46, 50, 53, 65, 68, 72,
  77, 82, 84–86, 88, 117
  background 50
  diversity 16
  factors 17, 22, 66
  forces 21, 123, 148
  implications 37, 65
  influences 50, 65, 72, 82
  pressures 18, 23
  resources 10, 65, 84
  status 7, 8, 12, 17, 50, 67, 70
Eder, Donna 50, 51, 61, 78, 79, 84,
  111

Education,
   multicultural 10–12, 33, 67,
      130, 133
   progressive 23, 93
Educational jargon 68
Effective[ness] 31, 60, 117, 125
   middle schools 28, 30, 31, 56, 81
   practices 119
   strategies 108, 125
   teaching 42
Eichhorn, Donald 30
Egocentrism 43
Elkind, Donald 28
Emotional development 12, 30, 32, 42–
   44
*Emotional Intelligence: Why It Can Matter More
   than IQ* 26
Empower[ment]
   students 53, 67, 97, 100, 107
   teacher 31
English 13, 14, 46, 47, 64, 68, 71, 113
English as a Second Language [ESL] 68
English Language Learners [ELL] 68
Environment 125
   classroom 21, 41
   learning 7, 11, 21, 27, 32, 33, 36, 41,
      53, 57, 68, 71, 72, 75, 82, 93, 96,
      98, 99, 124, 131
   school 8, 18, 32, 16, 18, 36, 53, 78,
      96, 100
   socio-cultural 133
   supportive 56, 62, 76, 79, 80, 94,
      147
Erikson, Erik 24, 25, 27, 28, 41, 45, 49
Estomin, Lynn 92
Ethic issues 28, 30, 31, 120
Ethnic 11, 15, 37, 48, 51, 53
   diversity 15

forces 136
   groups 11, 16, 18, 47, 48, 64
   identity 47, 49, 64, 78
   influences 47, 63, 82
Ethnicity 10, 12, 16, 46–48, 50, 57,
   63, 64, 79, 123
Ethnocentrism 16
Euro American 27, 66, 47, 85
Expectations 10, 12, 18, 26, 28, 31,
   34, 45, 46, 60, 63, 64, 69, 70, 79,
   102, 110, 111, 130
   cultural 45, 46, 84
   high 28, 57, 64, 70
Experiences 7, 12, 15, 17, 18, 22, 26,
   33, 37, 40, 66, 92
   cultural 113
Exploratory courses 41, 90
Extracurricular 83, 100
Extrinsic 60, 61

F

Factors
   cultural 106
   economic 17, 22, 66
   political 22
   socio-economic 17, 29, 66
*Failing at Fairness: How America's Schools
   Cheat Girls* 45
Fair[ness] 8, 81, 103, 105
Feedback 113, 141
Feminis[t] 12, 25, 30, 37
   pedagogy 97, 103
   perspective 13, 35, 37
   theory 36, 98, 105
Field theory 26, 28
Finances 87, 140
   school 135

Financial support 119
Flexibility 32, 34–36, 91, 125, 129,
    130, 134
  organizational 137
Football 52, 99, 123
Forces 23
  economic 21, 123, 148
  ethnic 136
  group 9
  political 123, 148
  socio-economic 21, 136
Frame of reference, cultural 63, 67, 68
Freedom 26, 33, 51, 78
Freud, [Sigmund] 24, 28
Friend 6, 8, 17, 23, 24, 33, 40–42, 52,
    53, 56, 75, 106
Friendships 6, 75, 78, 85
  patterns 78
  same-sex 24
  cross-race 85
Future 7, 23, 25, 29, 37, 46, 107, 109,
    128, 129, 136, 139

G

Gangs 78, 79
Gardner, Howard 120, 134
Gay 13, 45, 46, 136
Gender 7, 9, 11-13, 18, 37, 44–46,
    50, 51, 53, 57, 63, 66, 77, 79, 80,
    83, 85, 99, 112, 113, 144
  bias 51
  differences 45, 72, 112, 113, 131
  issues 9, 45, 72, 112–114, 131
  perspectives 36
  relationships 83, 98
  research 86
  roles 46, 77, 84

studies 12
Gessell, Arnold 26, 29
Gilligan, Carol 27, 29, 45, 56
Girls 12-14, 42, 43, 45–47, 51, 52,
    62, 82–84, 99, 123, 136
Giroux, Henry 124, 137
Giver, The 101
Glasser, William 77, 78
Global
  community 15
  society 101, 118
Goals 11, 31, 59, 65, 66, 69, 90, 111,
    114, 131,141
Goleman, Daniel 26
Grades 55, 57, 59, 61, 113
Grant, Carl 10, 11
*Great Transitions: Preparing Adolescents for a
    New Century* 31, 115
Group 10–12, 14–17, 24, 28, 32, 41,
    43, 47–50, 78, 89, 84, 110
  cultural 11, 64, 48
  decision making 81
  dominant 87
  ethnic 11, 16, 18, 47, 48, 64
  heterogeneous 98, 111, 132
  group 6
  interaction 114
  norms 69
  parent 140
  peer 29, 45, 87, 91
  racial 11
  relationships 25
  social 8, 9
  student 76, 86, 96, 98, 131
  theory 111
Group Processes in the Classroom 111

H

Hall, G. Stanley 21
Hart, Elva T. 47
Havighurst, Robert 26, 29
Help 6, 31, 33, 34, 41, 53, 56, 57, 58, 71, 130
Heterogeneous group 98, 111, 132
High expectations 28, 57, 64, 70
High income 51
High standards 65, 70, 129, 135
Higher order thinking 123
Hinchey, Patricia 123
Historical 16, 21, 39, 68, 143
History 11, 15, 16, 36, 39, 49, 67, 101, 102
Homosexual[ity] 2, 45, 46, 83, 112, 145
Homework 6, 17, 104
Humor 81, 110, 113

I

Identit[ies] 6, 18, 25, 28, 29, 34, 35 39-50, 53, 89
achievement 41, 48
African American 46, 49, 63
biracial 50
Black student 49
development 25, 29, 33–35, 45–47, 49, 50, 53, 64, 72, 92
cultural 47, 67
ethnic 47, 49, 64, 78
group 6
multiple 19, 123
Identity v. Role confusion 25
Images, cultural 47, 67
Immigrants 13, 22, 49, 64
beliefs 64

Implications 45
economic 37, 65
Income 17
high 51
low 51, 70, 88, 89, 100, 136
Independence 30, 41, 44, 53
Industry 24, 25, 27
Industry v. Inferiority 24
Ineffective strategies 71
Influences 37
cultural 24, 36
economic 50, 65, 72, 82
ethnic 47, 63, 82
organizational 82
political 86
social 37, 72, 82, 85, 86
Institutions of higher learning 140
Instruction, differentiated 105
Intellectual
ability 26
development 12, 43, 44, 80
Interactions 26, 28, 29, 30
group 114
student-teacher 34, 45, 86, 88
parents 117
peer 84, 107
positive 80
Interdisciplinary team 6, 81, 95
Interests, student 36, 42, 90
Intergenerational relationships 82
Internet 17, 120, 136
Interpersonal relationships 26, 97, 135
Interpersonal skills 50, 96
Interpretations, cultural 80
Inter-racial marriages 9
Intrinsic 61
Invincibility fable 43
Islam 15, 102

Isolate 78, 79, 84

Issues 44, 45, 49, 51, 58, 92, 123
controversial 108
diversity 7, 9, 12, 18
ethical 28, 30, 31, 120
gender 9, 45, 72, 112–114, 131
political 123, 148
racial 51
social 12, 48, 92, 96, 120
socio-economic 44–46, 135

J

Jocks and Burnouts 88
Journals 113
Junior high 21, 22, 84, 119

K

Kincheloe, Joe 138
Knowing, Women's Way of 36
Knowledge 11, 12, 15, 18, 23, 25, 31,
33-37, 41, 48, 68, 69, 94, 95, 99,
125, 129, 133, 137, 138, 145, 146,
150
Kohlberg, Lawrence 13, 29, 105
Kohn, Alfie 60, 61
Kozol, Jonathan 5, 11, 65, 90, 95, 135

L

Ladson-Billings, Gloria 53, 63
Lakota Woman 48
Language 8–10, 11–14, 18, 36, 57, 64,
65, 112, 144, 147
native 11, 64
second 13, 65
Latina/Latino 46, 47

Leadership role 42

Learners
community of 18, 36, 93, 94,
97, 124, 146
role 93

Learning 7, 8, 10, 11, 18, 33, 35, 36
community 18, 21, 31, 33, 35, 36,
53, 92, 97, 103, 124
environment 7, 11, 21, 27, 32, 33,
36, 41, 53, 57, 68, 71, 72, 75,
82, 93, 96, 98, 99, 124, 131
strategies 95
styles 11, 147

Lesbian 13, 45, 46

Level
organizational 22, 139
socio-economic 69

Lewin, Kurt 26, 29

Lies My Teacher Told Me 37

Linguistic diversity 14, 46, 67, 68

Listen 19, 111, 114, 115, 121, 122,
133, 139

Listener 81

Literacy 66

Literature 11, 15, 27, 28, 32, 41, 44,
46, 57, 67, 82, 132, 140
biracial 15
middle school 7, 10, 19, 30, 33, 46
multicultural 11
multiracial 15

Loewen, James W. 37

Looping 132

Loving v. Virginia 15, 49

Low income 50, 70, 88, 89, 100, 136

Lower tracks 9, 50, 70

M

Management, classroom 103, 104
Marcia, James 47
Marriage
  biracial 15, 49
  inter-racial 9
Masculinity 13, 62
Materials, differentiated 134
Mathematics 44, 145
Maturational theory 26, 29
Media 66, 144
Mead, Margaret 25–27, 29, 84,
Message, 45, 85, 66, 89, 90, 99, 105,
  113, 114, 122, 135
Methods, differentiated 134
Middle Eastern culture 143
Middle school
  concept 22, 23, 31
  development 21, 23
  effective 30, 31, 56, 81
  literature 7, 10, 19, 30, 33, 46
  philosophy 9, 13, 18, 19, 25, 34, 111
  purpose 28
  qualities 31, 32
Minority 10
  model 64
  students 9, 49, 70, 76, 85, 132, 133,
  136
Mistrust, cultural 87
Model
  minority 64
  role 15, 80, 94, 142
Modeling 76
Moos, Rudolph 33–35
Moral
  decisions 13
  development 12, 13, 29, 30

Motivation 60, 141, 146
Multicultural
  education 10–12, 33, 67, 130
    133
  literature 14, 46, 67, 68
Multiethnic 50
Multilingual 11, 68
Multiple identities 19, 123
Multiple intelligences 130, 134
Multiracial children 12
Multiracial 49, 50
  literature 15
Muslims 15
Myths 115, 116, 128, 129, 135, 139

N

National Association of Secondary School
  Principals [NASSP] 19, 30, 31, 44
Nationalism 101
National Middle School Association
  [NMSA] 19, 30–31, 43, 56, 61, 91,
  93, 94, 97
National standards 23
Nation at Risk, A 31
Native Americans 13, 47–49, 50, 62,
  86, 144
Native languages 11, 13, 113
Needs 17, 22, 24, 28, 31–33, 37
  adolescent 12, 17, 19, 22–24, 28, 30,
    31, 37, 137, 30
  developmental 12, 22, 24, 31, 63, 69,
    70
  students 12, 13, 22, 37, 46, 53, 113,
    131, 132
  society 12, 23–25, 37, 137
New World Order 101
No Child Left Behind 130

Noddings, Nel 6, 32, 53, 89, 97, 107

No Justice, No Peace 92

Nonverbal communication 114

Norms 14, 102, 103, 111

  cultural 63

  group 69

O

Ogbu, John 49, 78

Open enrollment program 136

Opinions 8, 32, 50, 96.98, 99, 101,
106, 111, 117, 118, 121, 122, 136,
142

  student 98, 99, 104, 107

Oprah 45

Organizations 19, 27, 28, 30–32, 75,
95

  community 97

Organization, school 10, 21, 22, 35

Organizational 32

  change 139

  flexibility 137

  influences 82

  level 22, 139

  patterns 131

  system 103

Ownership 92, 95

P

Pandora 128

Parent 13, 14, 17, 18, 24, 25, 29, 30,
44, 48, 50, 51, 68, 88, 90, 115, 117

  beliefs 48, 100

  conference 6, 17, 18, 68, 113, 115,
116, 155

  group 140

interactions 117

  role 117

Participation 15, 16, 24, 25, 34, 36, 78,
88, 89, 92, 93, 95, 98, 99

Patterns

  friendship 78

  organizational 131

Pedagogy

  feminist 97, 103

Peer 30, 42, 43, 50, 96, 112, 119, 137

  acceptance 61

  approval 4

  groups 29, 45, 87, 91

  interactions 84, 107

  relationships 25, 32, 33, 41, 43, 49,
50, 63, 81, 90

  status 112

Perceptions 7, 13, 15, 27, 33, 36, 41,
43, 45–47, 49, 65, 102, 139

  student 7, 43, 45, 47, 50, 56, 70–72,
92, 134

Personal development 34, 35, 56

Perspectives 7, 9–11, 13, 14, 21, 27,
37, 99, 124

  cultural 59, 65

  feminist 13, 35, 37

  gender 36

  political 36

  racial 36

Philosophy, middle school 9, 13, 18, 19,
25, 34

Phinney,[Jean] 47, 48

Physical development 112, 30, 32, 42–
44

Pipher, Margaret 45

Pluralism, cultural 11

Pluralistic society 98, 107

Political
  activism 8
  climate 87
  factors 22
  forces 123, 148
  influences 86
  issues 46, 118, 144
  perspective 36
  system 108
Politicians 130
Politics 92, 118
Pollack, William 12, 45, 62
Popularity 61, 62, 88
Positive interactions 80
Postmodern 36, 37
Poverty 65, 89
Power 21, 22, 31, 36, 37, 45, 50, 67,
  68, 77–79, 82, 83–84, 87, 93–99,
  105, 117, 125,136, 137,
  relationships 85, 137
  systems 79, 93, 125, 133
Practices
  classroom 14, 15, 103, 104
  effective 119
Prejudice 8, 9, 18, 52,
Pre-service teachers 115, 145, 147
Pressures
  economic 18, 23
Principal 7, 14, 76, 96, 114, 119
Problem-based learning 80, 123
Professional[ism] 6, 18, 19, 23, 53, 75,
  97, 118–120, 131, 138-140
Progressive education 23, 93
Pseudo-participation 107
Psychoanalytic theory 24, 25, 28
Psycho-social theory 28, 30, 43
Puberty 24, 42

*Punished by Rewards: The Trouble with Gold
  Stars, Incentive Plans, A's, Praise and Other
  Bribes* 60
Punishment 10 3
Purpose of middle level education 28
Purpose of schools 32, 128

Q

Qualitative research 130
Qualities of middle schools 31, 32

R

Race 8, 9, 12, 15, 16, 18, 36, 51, 57,
  58, 79, 82, 85, 87, 98
Racial 8, 9, 11, 15, 47, 53
  diversity 15, 44, 85
  group 11
  issues 51
  perspective 36
  relationships 98
Racism 15, 49, 100
Real Boys 12
*Real Boys' Voices: Rescuing Our Sons from the
  Myths of Boyhood* 12, 13
Reality of school 66, 130
Real-life 61, 93, 107, 117, 123, 133
Reflect 5, 16, 31, 37,141, 147
Reflections 12, 18, 53, 56, 101
Rejection 40, 79, 99
Relationships 7, 11, 13, 15, 25–27, 30,
  32–35, 41–43, 49, 50, 61, 62, 71,
  72, 75–79, 82-86, 90, 96, 100
  group 25
  intergenerational 82
  interpersonal 26, 97, 135

Relationships (cont)
  peer 25, 32, 33, 41, 43, 49, 50, 63,
    81, 90
  power 85, 137
  student 6, 7, 72, 73, 77–79, 84, 88,
    95, 98, 125, 132
  gender 83, 98
Relevant, culturally 63, 86–88, 132,
  134, 147
Religion 10, 12, 14–16, 46
Religious 8, 14, 15, 44, 136
  Diversity 8, 10, 14
Research 7, 10, 13, 23, 39, 45, 46, 50,
  140, 142
  critical action 130
  gender 86
qualitative 130
Resources
  economic 10, 65, 84
Respect 7, 16, 18, 32, 33, 45, 46, 76,
  79–81, 89, 96, 97, 99, 100, 102,
  104, 110, 111, 125, 132
Responsibility 8, 30, 46, 95, 128, 129,
  139
Responsive
  culturally 68, 75, 76, 87, 88, 96,
    99, 105, 108, 109, 111, 117,
    133, 135, 146
  developmentally 32, 35, 37, 42, 47,
    53, 70, 99, 105, 108, 109, 111,
    121, 137
Reviving Ophelia: Saving the Selves of Adolescent
  Girls 45
Rewards 60, 61, 81, 103
Rights 9, 94, 100, 102, 103
Role[s] 12, 16, 24–26, 30, 34, 40-43,
  45–47, 49, 66, 83, 84, 94, 142,
  gender 46, 77, 84

leadership 42
model 15, 80, 94, 142
learner 93
parent 117
school 102
societ[al] 12, 25
student 99, 125
teacher 130
Rules 18, 34, 52, 62, 63, 89, 90, 100,
  102, 103, 105, 106

S

Sadker, David and Myra 12, 45, 62
Same-sex friendships 82
Savage Inequalities: Children in America's
  Schools 91
Scheduling 90
School
  climate 30, 35, 90, 124
  community 16, 19, 34, 36, 53, 65,
    72, 85, 87, 94, 95, 100, 102, 103,
    110, 115
  culture 123
  democratic 63, 92, 103
  environment 8, 16, 18, 36, 53, 78,
    96, 100
  finance 135
  organization 10, 21, 22, 31
  purpose of 32, 128
  supportive 65, 116
  system 102, 135
Schooling 6, 129
School Talk: Gender and Adolescent Culture
  111
Science 23, 65, 91
Second language 13, 64
Secular trend 27, 84

Security 24, 80
Segregation 8, 9, 83
Self 23, 25–27, 30, 34, 40, 41, 48,
   50, 53
Self-concept 41, 50
Self-image 40, 50
Selman, [Robert] 24, 26, 30
Sense of community 107
Sergiovanni, Thomas 35
Service, community 97, 100–102
Sexist 51 52, 112
   bias 112
Shor, Ira 63, 105, 123
Sleeter, Christine 10, 11
Social 8, 11, 13, 16, 18, 24–26, 30,
   33, 37, 50
   action 11, 12, 33, 67
   class 11, 36, 50, 79, 88, 123
   development 12, 30, 43
   groups 8, 9
   influences 37, 72, 82, 85, 86
   issues 12, 48, 92, 96, 120
   system 30
Societal 12
   attitudes 136
   needs 12, 23, 24, 37, 137
   roles 12, 25
Society 9, 10, 12–16, 18, 23–25, 30,
   37
   democratic 95, 99
   global 101, 118
   pluralistic 98, 107
   role 122
Socio-cultural environment 133
Socio-economic 24
   differences 46, 131
   factors 17, 29, 66
   forces 21, 136

groups 9
   issues 44–46, 135
   levels 69
   status 8, 12, 17, 67
Sports 51, 52
Sputnik 23, 128
Stakeholders 7, 35, 99, 101, 102, 108
   109
Standardized tests 70, 130, 135
Standards 23, 20, 29, 59, 60, 92
   high 65, 70, 129, 135
   national 23
Standards movement 70, 130, 135
Status 8, 17, 23, 25, 45, 50, 82, 84, 88
   economic 7, 8, 12, 17, 50, 67, 70
   peer. 112
   socio-economic 8, 12, 17, 67
Stereotypes 11, 64, 68, 83, 133
Strategies
   effective 108, 125
   ineffective 71
   learning 95
Student(s)
   Asian 65, 133
   beliefs 50, 79, 86, 88, 109, 123
   biracial 15
   diverse 48, 53, 67, 85, 131, 132
   empowerment 53, 67, 97, 100, 107
   interests 36, 42, 90
   groups 76, 86, 96, 98, 131
   minority 49, 70, 76, 85, 132, 133,
      136
   needs 12, 13, 53, 65, 70, 94, 133,
      142
   opinions 98, 99, 104, 107
   perceptions 7, 43, 45, 47, 50, 56,
      70–72, 92, 134
   roles 99, 125

Students (cont)
teacher interactions 71
  relationships 72, 73, 77–79, 84, 88,
    95, 98, 125, 132
Student-teacher interactions 34, 45, 86,
  88
Studies
  gender 12
  Women's 11
Styles, learning 11, 147
Subcultures 79
Success 10, 12–14, 18, 25, 27, 31-36,
  49, 53, 56, 57, 60, 62, 63, 66, 71,
  72, 81, 87, 131, 135, 141, 142,
  145, 146
  academic 61, 63–65, 68, 69
  barriers 10
Supportive
  community 37, 93, 114, 134
  environment 56, 62, 76, 79, 80, 94,
    147
  schools 65, 116
System[s] 8, 12, 30, 34, 35, 37, 50, 55,
  76, 104, 107, 112
  belief 94
  organizational 103
  political 108
  power 79, 93, 125, 133
  school 102, 135
  social 30
  theory 97, 111, 130

T

Talk 7, 14, 18, 89, 109, 110, 119, 133
Teachable moment 26
Teacher
  attitudes 32, 40, 53

beliefs 115
  certification 23, 135
  empowerment 31
  role 130
Teaching
  effective 42
Team 6, 64, 80, 111, 119
  interdisciplinary 6, 81, 95
Teamwork 95
Technology 17, 36, 117, 120, 130, 136
Tensions 98, 99, 134
Thematic approach 41, 64, 133
Theor[ies] 32
  community 7, 98, 130, 148
  critical 37, 130, 137, 145
  curriculum 9
  development 24, 27–30, 45, 131
  group 76, 86, 96, 98, 131
  feminist 36, 98, 105
  field 26, 28
  maturational 26, 29
  psychoanalytic 24, 25, 29
  psycho-social 29, 30, 43
  system 97, 111, 130
Tests, standardized 70, 130, 135
Textbooks 10, 45, 65
Thinking 6, 11, 43, 44, 123
  abstract 44, 45, 57, 69
  concrete 44, 57, 69
  critical 118, 129
  higher order 123
This We Believe: Developmentally Responsive
Middle Schools 30
Time 6–10, 12, 15, 16, 18, 48, 49, 51,
  52
Track[ing] 9, 50, 132
  lower 9, 50, 70
Transition 24, 26

Trust 33, 86, 90

*Turning Points: Educating Adolescents for the 21st
    Century* 138

*Turning Points: Preparing American Youth for
    the 21st Century* 31, 102, 138

U

Urban 111

V

Values 7, 14, 16, 19, 24, 30, 40–42,
    78, 94, 124

Vision 28, 30, 37, 38, 66, 119, 136,
    140, 146, 148

Vocabulary 58, 104, 110

Vouchers 135

W

Wars, culture 98

Whiteness 15, 46

Women's studies 11

Working-class 18

Words 9, 10, 14, 110–112

X

X-Mod 6, 110

Y

Youth culture 42, 81, 94, 124

Studies in the Postmodern Theory of Education

General Editors
Joe L. Kincheloe & Shirley R. Steinberg

Counterpoints publishes the most compelling and imaginative books being written in education today. Grounded on the theoretical advances in criticalism, feminism, and postmodernism in the last two decades of the twentieth century, Counterpoints engages the meaning of these innovations in various forms of educational expression. Committed to the proposition that theoretical literature should be accessible to a variety of audiences, the series insists that its authors avoid esoteric and jargonistic languages that transform educational scholarship into an elite discourse for the initiated. Scholarly work matters only to the degree it affects consciousness and practice at multiple sites. Counterpoints' editorial policy is based on these principles and the ability of scholars to break new ground, to open new conversations, to go where educators have never gone before.

For additional information about this series or for the submission of manuscripts, please contact:

> Joe L. Kincheloe & Shirley R. Steinberg
> c/o Peter Lang Publishing, Inc.
> 275 Seventh Avenue, 28th floor
> New York, New York 10001

To order other books in this series, please contact our Customer Service Department:

> (800) 770-LANG (within the U.S.)
> (212) 647-7706 (outside the U.S.)
> (212) 647-7707 FAX

Or browse online by series:

> www.peterlangusa.com